Anthony Murray

What Happened To Your
DREAMS?

A Guide To Rekindling and Restoring
Dreams Lost or Forgotten

*Ms. Pat
have you
Dream Big*

OASIS Family Life Church
210 Paulding Lane
Dallas, GA 30132

Some names and identifying details have been changed to protect the privacy of individuals.

ISBN-13: 978-0615685823
ISBN-10: 061568582X

Book Cover, Interior Design and Layout by Chaun Archer - AVIDMultimedia.net

Published by OASIS Family Life Church
Printed in the United States of America.

First Edition

10 9 8 7 6 5 4 3 2 1

DEDICATION

To my parents for sowing seeds of faith and courage to pursue my dreams, and my wife for watering them with prayer, patience, trust, and sacrifice.

TABLE OF CONTENTS

INTRODUCTION

One of your greatest assets is your active imagination founded in what God says about you. You can't believe in God without engaging your imagination.

What Happened to Your Dreams is a lesson in using your imagination to reach higher than the stars. Why reach for the stars when the universe is so much bigger?

"Now unto Him who can do exceeding abundantly above all that you can ask or think according to the power that works in you," (Ephesians 3:30). God is able to do more than you can even ask Him for. Why settle for mediocrity when you can have your biggest dream come true. He has given you the power to go far beyond what you can even imagine.

"Imagination is the facility to form new ideas in the brain. It is the means to use resourcefulness to solve unusual and difficult problems. Albert Einstein said, "Imagination is more important than knowledge."

In your imaginations lie limitless possibilities. Don't reject any thought that will take you higher than where you are now. Those thoughts belong in the arena that will take you to the place prepared for you.

If you have not been able to grasp the loftiness of what God has for you, start meditating on the great and imagining the best until you do. Do not make jokes about your future or belittle your dreams. If you are honest with yourself, what you are really doing is trying to get someone to agree with your doubt or someone to quiet your fears.

I once heard the story of a runner who passed an elderly man fishing at a local lake every day. He would greet the man and keep on running. He sometimes noticed that the man would catch a great fish and toss it back into the lake. The runner decided that he would have to ask about the tossing.

One day the runner left home a little earlier so that he could stop and have a conversation with the elderly man. When he reached the lake, the man was not there. This troubled the runner, because he had been passing him for the better part of a year.

Months later, the runner ran across the man at the local gas station. He was so overjoyed, he wanted to hug him. He settled on a smile and a hardy handshake. Then he asked, "What happened to your daily fishing at the lake?"

The man responded, "You know, it was really pleasant for many months. There were plenty of fish to go around, and I ate for many months on the fish I caught. Then I found myself having to throw back those gigantic fish.

"I was talking to the gentleman where I buy my bait. He informed me that the lake owners had decided to start stocking the lake with bigger fish to attract more anglers. Well, I just have a small frying pan. Those big ole fish couldn't fit in it. I found a small fishing hole across town. That's where I go now."

"Why didn't you just buy a bigger frying pan?" the runner asked.

"Wow, I never thought of that!"

Is your frying pan too small? If so, you have to enlarge your mind to conceive what God has for you. The old man did not have a lack of blessings; he had not prepared for blessings. You can't wait till the blessings start coming in to plan for them. If you have not asked for more, believed for more, or expected more, you will not recognize when more comes.

That's right. More can be right at your doorstep, but you may not have been looking for it. You may not recognize it because it may just come in the form of power to receive wealth.

Of course you can recognize money when it comes. But money is not wealth. Wealth is the accumulation of assets. What other assets is God trying to get to you—but you have not dreamed big enough?

As a seed of Abraham (Acts 3:26), you are expected not only to be blessed, but also to be a blessing, just as he was. Expand your dreaming to include the blessing of others. It does not matter where you find yourself right now, you can go higher. Dream bigger. Since you know that God is going to exceed the abundance of your imagination, why start at the sky? You can see that! There is no limit. Open your mind to receive the dream that God is willing to give you.

There is always something to work on, always a dream that has not been conquered. God began the work and has the authority and power to finish it. Your

WHAT HAPPENED TO YOUR DREAMS?

faith is not in yourself, but in an all-powerful God. Dream really big!

As you read, remember you are going where you have never gone before. If your dream is a future that you can make happen yourself, it's not big enough. Expect great things. Look for manifestation of the impossible.

Impossible things are happening every day. Why not let them happen for you?

PART

1

Who Are You?
Really?

BORN TO INSPIRE

1

"All of us are born for a reason, but all of us don't discover why."

\- Danny Thomas

Right this moment I am living my dream. Although my dream has prospered me and causes great thanksgivings to God, my greatest joy is in my ability to inspire others.

When I first started as a pastor, I knew that building leadership was my passion. While teenagers were being addressed as hos and drug dealers, I spoke to them in a positive light. These kids were from the ghetto, projects and were thrown away. Others spoke negative in their life, I spoke positive. I sent out letters to newcomers and visitors and I addressed them to community leaders. That trend was a staple of my entire tenure as a youth pastor. Out of the first fifty youth that attended the Monday night service, seven or eight of them developed into leaders that helped direct and inspire the hundreds that would come.

The purpose of ministry is to inspire others to change the things in their lives that keep them from achieving their God-given potential—the kind of potential that feeds dreams and does great feats.

You are made in the image and likeness of God. No matter how far you stray away, there is always a draw inside of you saying, "Do the right thing." As the image of God, you have to go out of your way not to do the right thing.

By the mere essence of who He is, God is a giver. From the day of creation until now, God continues to give. For every action you take, God guarantees a reaction.

As a leader, God has placed in me the desired skills to inspire followers. People do not follow me because I'm Anthony Murray; they follow God in me. My responsibility is to nurture the seeds of what I am called to do.

These attributes also belong to you. God has called you to be great. God knew what you would be before He placed you in your mother's womb (Jeremiah 1:8). Your job is to grow into who you are called to be and to inspire others to do the same.

One of the constants that I heard in the early days of pastoring is the plea from new converts to know their purpose. I believe that tapping into your gifts is not the far-off, mystical experience that you may believe. You just have to go confidently into the direction of your dreams.

One sermon that blessed my life early on was "Doing the Work of the Ministry Defines Who You Are." God gave that to me, and it inspired many who adhered to its call. You just have to obey the pull from within, no matter how far you are from your desires. Just know that God put the desires there. All you have to do is start. Do something for somebody else.

DREAMSPIRATION

Jean Jackson is a registered nurse in New York City. She works in one of the most prestigious cancer treatment hospitals in the nation. As a child, she loved playing doctor. A set of medical journals that her mother received as a child found their way into Jean's hands. Jean was one of eight children living in one of the oldest housing projects in the city, right at the foot of the East River. Her siblings were her constant "patients." At their bedsides, she attended to their needs and diagnosed their ailments. Of course this was all in her vivid imagination.

Ever since she was a child Jean knew that she would go to college. She spent several summers in a program catering to underprivileged, gifted children at the illustrious Columbia University. She later went on to a college out of state to major in nursing.

Today, Jean has an administrative position at the hospital and earns a six-figure income. As the eldest child, she inspired most of her siblings to get degrees and excel in their careers. Neither of her parents were college graduates, but there was a foundation for learning embedded in Jean's makeup.

Jean also raised her children to do their best. They both graduated

DREAMSPIRATION

from Ivy League schools, as Jean funded their education with her salary and overtime. They both lead prosperous and dream-realized lives and careers.

It didn't matter that Jean grew up poor and was not encouraged to further her education. She made up her mind to dream and dream big. Her dream has inspired her siblings, her children, and her nieces and nephews. She singlehandedly broke the chain of poverty that she grew up in. She accepted the call on her life to be a trailblazer.

Jean remains a leader in her family. She plans family vacations with her siblings and gives open-heartedly whenever the opportunity presents itself. She tends to the needs of family members who get sick, even traveling out of state to do it.

This story is not meant to entertain you. It is meant to show that there is room for every one of God's people to reach higher than they have ever gone before. Your goal should be to inspire others. You were not put on this earth to live on a deserted island. The universe is waiting for your gift to shine. Someone is watching you. What are you preparing to do?

Be honest with yourself. You have a desire deep within you to be an influence to someone. Your life force is calling for you to take action. You will either foster thoughts or feelings that encourage a change for the better or for the negative. Decide to jump on the better wagon. Being a true inspiration requires work. But the benefits are worth the effort.

Desire to inspire and you will not be able to keep it from yourself!

Questions?

Who Inspires You and Why?

Are You an Inspiration to others? Why or Why Not?

What are some things that you can do to inspire the people around you?

What do you believe is your purpose?

What work are you involved in at church or in your community?

WHAT ARE YOU DREAMING ABOUT?

"Go confidently in the direction of your dreams. Live the life you have imagined."
- Henry David Thoreau

Everybody dreams. Not those crazy thoughts that haunt your sleep because you ate a pot of cabbage at midnight. I am talking about those reoccurring scenes where you are living high above the state of your current life. Those thoughts come to mind and bring exhilarating feelings of joy and contentment, often followed by feelings of anxiety and fear.

Dreams do not only happen in a state of slumber or unconsciousness; they are the innermost hopes and desires of what your ultimate life would be. They are visions of the life God intended you to have—with more joy and contentment, and less worry, doubt, fear, shame, and lack.

Each person has his or her own dream. Although some people's dreams may be similar to yours, God has designed a unique plan and path for your life. These dreams are not a fantasy, but an introduction to a road on which God wants you to embark. God-inspired dreams work out every time, so do not be discouraged about your path. Your steps are ordered by God.

Let me help you think about this in depth so you can grab hold of the direction of this book. Your life will be revolutionized, and you will begin to fulfill the purpose for which you were put on this earth.

Do you believe that you don't have a dream? There are many reasons for this. You may have suppressed your dream because it was too enormous to fit into your uninspired lifestyle. You could not even begin to imagine a life so fulfilled.

Life with no hope has a way of zapping your desire to accomplish more. When all you can think of is survival, how can you work on a dream that would give you a life that's 150 percent better than the one you live now?

Survival mode is the state the majority of people live in. It is called "an average life." Unfortunately, it is not the life God has planned for you. He said in John 10:10 that, "He came that you may have life and life more abundantly." I ask you again, what are you dreaming about? Sit for a minute and concentrate on that question, and then answer it honestly.

What if I don't have a dream?

God has a plan just for you. In the book of Jeremiah, we see a young man despondent about the plight of his people. God stopped him in his tracks and said, "Before I formed you in the womb I knew you, before you were born I set you apart, I appointed you as a prophet to the nations" (Jeremiah 1:5). God was telling him that his life was meant for more than despair. God created Jeremiah to encourage, exalt, and correct God's people.

When you are struggling and can't see your way or when your dream seems impossible, remember God knew you before you were formed in your mother's womb, and with Him, you can do the impossible.

Nothing escapes the mind of God. If you are afraid to change, do not be. God has a remedy. He said in His Word that He will never leave you nor forsake you (Hebrews 13:5), so you can rest assured that He will be with you every step of the way.

Change is hard, but it is necessary. Change is the one constant in your life. Being open to change will help you continuously stay in the system in which God operates. God's system is like a lazy river at a water park. Just get in with your tube, and let the current pull you in the direction you need to go. The lazy river at the water park was designed as a place to rest and relax. In the same way, God's system allows you to rest and relax in Him.

Trust God. Remember, He does not want to do you any harm. He only wants good for you. No matter how scary change seems to you, God has given you the authority to make the positive changes needed to bless your life.

Wanting to know everything in advance can hinder your dreams from coming into reality. I have this problem. I get so excited with my God-given dreams I begin to ask God the W's: who, what, where, why, and when. I am like a child getting on a parent's nerve the day before his birthday. I know God is going to do what He planned, but I am so excited about my dreams that I believe I am ready now. God has to help me slow down my mind, because there is always a process before I can get to the finished picture. There is a journey I must take.

Each journey has hills and valleys, nooks and crannies, and giants we must face. A journey is a marathon, not a sprint. I can't allow my impatient actions to get in the way of God's plan. Adam and Eve did this in the Garden. They let their curiosity and impatience get in the way of their destiny. God had given Adam and Eve tasks to do to occupy their minds and bodies. But they were not satisfied with those tasks; they wanted to know more. Because of this, they fell into sin. God is so good, He had a plan for their redemption. His plan was to get them back to His original plan of relationship with Him.

Remember that God's plan to give you the good always reappears after the bad. He cursed all of mankind because of Adam and Eve's sin; then He redeemed man with the blood of His son, Jesus. This redemption is here for you today. There is a way for you to be redeemed after you have veered off of the plan for your life. Get back on the right road and be redeemed from the consequences of your wrong choices.

As we read more into the story of Jeremiah we see an encouragement coming from God right in the middle of despair. God says to Jeremiah, "For I know the plans I have for you...plans to prosper you and not to harm you, plans to give you hope and a future," (Jeremiah 29:11). God has the same thoughts toward you. What would be the purpose of you living in mediocrity? Doing great things gives God glory, and it is what He wants. God wants to do great things in the earth through you. Embrace this reality, and start dreaming bigger.

How do I know my dreams are from God? you may be asking right now. This is revealed only when you are moving in the correct direction for your life. Allow me to explain each of them:

1. The first character trait of Godly dreaming is that you will always be goal oriented. If your imagination is telling you that what you are dreaming will bring overnight success, send it back. Goals not only keep you motivated but when achieved bring victory at every level. Goals are continuously added and keep you moving forward.

Ǫ Failures are not a deterrent to the dreamer. Failures are a reminder of your faith and dependence on God. If you never make a mistake how can you relate to those who do? What kind of help are you to others? I do not have to emphasize this too much because if you are a true dreamer (or human) you have and will always have failures. You have already had some!

Ǫ Dreamers see the good in every situation. There is always a silver lining behind every dark cloud. You have an assurance of victory. Thoughts of quitting are never permanent.

Ǫ Finally, dreamers know that haters are part of the process. Haters let you know that you are doing the right thing. Keep it moving.

● ●

These next few paragraphs have been extremely difficult to write. I will not dare insult your intelligence by thinking that you are dull of understanding. You picked up this book because you want a change. For the following words to inspire you to pick up your dreams, you have to follow them with your faith.

I want to articulate a principle that is missed many times, and when it's missed, maturity stagnates. Yes, we do get older, have jobs, pay bills, buy houses, have children, and so on. But our life is built for so much more. Wherever you are on your personal road, it is time to expand. God is calling for those who will dream again.

God lives in a place called eternity, which may be explained as a continuous mass or stream. Eternity can only be understood by faith because it is God's domain. You live here on earth, where all things eventually come to an end, including your physical life. Your domain is in time. It is in eternity where God creates and perfects everything that you will ever know. After the work is complete, God speaks it into time.

God knew all the heavens before they existed. He spoke them into existence, saying, "Let there be light!"

Time is where you live. Eternity is not controlled, but simply exists. Time is controlled by eternity. God controls everything in time. Time was created by God to bring structure to your life. Time separates days, months, years, decades, and centuries. If there was no time, everything would live in eternity.

When anything is perfected by God in eternity and then placed in time, it is up to you to give the thing life. But if you do not know what authority you have on earth, then all that God has prepared for you will go unused by you.

You were created for greatness. God wants to do you good and not evil. How can you make an impact here on earth in your own surroundings, as well as influencing the lives of those around you, if you do not tap into the greatness God has given you?

If you are in a negative cycle, it will stop your destiny toward greatness, so it is time to get out. Life that continues in the same circle for years is not God's design for you. You can lie to yourself, but God knows the truth because He is truth. He continuously troubles your spirit with a prodding to do more.

Maybe you had a dream when you were younger. Maybe you dreamed of being a pilot, nurse, teacher, soldier, doctor, or even a millionaire. Here it is years later, and you are wondering about all the time that has elapsed.

If you sit quietly long enough, you will discover the dream is still there, lying dormant beneath all the average life you have lived. It's there waiting to be awakened. There is no life in it because you have not spoken to it, ever. You tell yourself that if no one knows, you will not have to explain when a goal does not work. If you keep quiet, you will not have to tell those supporters why you are not doing anything with it. Then, of course, you will not have to be concerned with haters you see tormenting others. Well, that last statement is not true. You will have haters regardless of your status in life.

There is one thing I know about predestination: whether you acknowledge a dream or not, it is oozing out of who you are. When I was a hotheaded teenager engaging in all I was big enough to do, leadership manifested wherever I went. I had a crew that followed me whenever I said, "Let's go!" No matter where it was: the club, the dollar movie, skating, and even church. My crew would fight with me and for me. When my life was arrested by God, my crew deserted me. But God gave me a new crew who wants the same thing that I want—all that God has. And we are going in the same direction. This crew is better, a new, improved crew.

If God can use you even when you do not acknowledge your dream, just get a mental picture of what it will be like when you do start walking in your dream, add some goals, and share with some supporters. These are the seeds of great success.

Only the truth has the ability to make you free. I am not telling you to yell your passiveness about dreaming to the world. Tell it to yourself, and shake it off. Get some paper and write down what you are dreaming about. Accept the plan for your life, and then tell it to someone else. Get with people who are going your way, and hop on board. Make some goals that include risks. God's got you. You cannot fail.

Your dream is waiting on you. It is time to catch up. God never changes

His mind about His plan for your life. Be determined to fulfill your purpose. Good things are waiting on you. The day you get inspired, do something. Tomorrow seems to always have allies—a whole lot more tomorrows. Decide today that you will dream again. Yes, that dream was for you and still is.

You do not have to know anything; that is what faith is for. The foundation of what inspires you is the evidence that your dream is real. See it, and walk toward it.

"Now faith is the substance of things hoped for the evidence of things not seen."

- Hebrews 11:1

Questions?

What are you dreaming about?
Do you know your gift, passion, or calling? What is it?
What's stopping you?

GROWING IN THE GUTTER

3

"We are all in the gutter, but some of us are looking at the stars."

— Oscar Wilde

You ask the question "How can I go after my dream when my current situation is a nightmare?" My answer is, "Even weeds grow in the gutter." The determination that a weed has to survive is the same determination many of us have to achieve our dreams. God is able to do more than what we can even dream of. When you are determined and you activate your faith to make your dreams come alive, you encounter the greatness of God.

Maybe you did not grow up in a mansion; maybe you did. Maybe you grew up poor, and you are fighting every day to come out of poverty. Maybe you had everything handed to you. In either case, you're in the gutter.

The gutter is not a physical place; it's a state of mind. We create a place in our mind that sometimes makes it difficult for our dreams to grow; and if we are not careful, it kills our determination.

Unforgiveness, self-hate, believing the lies you were told about yourself, past experiences, past failures, bad relationships, abuse, guilt—these things and others like them live in the gutter. They form a mental blockage that prevents you from wanting to pursue your dreams. You must be willing and determined to push past these things if you are going to make it.

What is hindering your dream? Let the wind blow you to fertile soil. Do not be afraid of the direction your dream is taking you. You have to trust that your end will be greater than your beginning. Dreams sometimes take you out of your comfort zone. But the life inside the dream is worth the struggle.

If you walk down a city street and look down at the cracks along the curb, you see grass from the seeds that have refused to die. Blown and tossed in the wind, they landed in the gutter. There they lay until, watered by rain and standing water, they grew.

I remember preaching in the cafeteria of Hiram High School, in Paulding County, GA. The congregation had begun to grow and do well: my wife, two daughters, and twelve others were faithful members of Oasis Family Life Church. While I spoke, I heard a still small voice reminding me of my dream. It was time to move. God was ready for Oasis Family Life Church to explore the next level of the dream. I could have comfortably stayed where I was, but my dream had not reached its full potential. I was not where God showed me I would be.

With no leads and no money, I started searching for land. Within a few miles of the high school was a twenty-year-old metal building sitting in a field with no pavement. Grass and weeds grew around the gravel and rocks. Inside there was no carpet or air-conditioning. It was just an old, rusty shell. This did not resemble my dream in the least, but it had the potential to be something great. In unison my wife and I exclaimed, "It's perfect!"

You have to understand that dreams never start out the way they end. We renovated the building, and most would never know what it was like when we first got here. After several phases of expansion and renovation, many people said we should just be happy with what we had and stop. "Look at what God has done," they'd say. But I had a responsibility to see the dream all the way through. I believe God, and until a dream that is given to me by Him is fully revealed, I won't stop.

There are millions of people who have believed in dreaming and walked from dream into reality. This is not hype. You were born for more than you currently see. You have to pick your dream back up or start dreaming. It is never too late. If you are five or one hundred, it does not matter Dreams have power. You can have a vision and get inspired, but dreams give you the details on how to get to that grand vision.

Why is it that some of us achieve great success with our dreams, and others seem to fail? The difference is the determination of a weed. Many people quit when they get knocked down or face an unexpected obstacle or decision, but failure is not in the fall. Failure happens when you refuse to get back up and keep trying. Never allow anything to block your path. So many times I've wanted to quit. There are times when I even felt justified in quitting, but my purpose has not been completely fulfilled.

Along with several other pastors and their wives, Christina and I went on a mission trip to the East African country of Kenya with an organization called Compassion International. I am going to attempt to describe the living conditions of the people in the slums there. It literally took my breath away.

Six hundred thousand people live on a tract of land in a six-mile radius. Their living quarters didn't compare to any poverty-stricken neighborhood I've ever visited. There was no running water, no bathrooms, and no floors. Domestic and wild animals were everywhere, sharing space with the people.

I studied these deplorable conditions and wondered, How can a dream live here?

A boy living in that Kenyan slum left a lasting impression on me. As we talked with the children, we asked what they wanted to be when they grew up. This young boy said, "A doctor." Reconciling what I know about dreaming with his words, I felt the power of compassion overcome me, and I vowed to support his dream.

One Sunday morning, soon after arriving back home, I was walking across the parking lot to the church. I looked up to see some grass growing on the roof. My first thought was to get maintenance to pull it out. Immediately my thoughts were detained and taken back to the state of the people I saw in Kenya. Instantaneously the thought came: "A dream can live anywhere!"

One crucial element of the dream-to-reality process is the power of the spoken word. You have to speak your dream out. Dreams locked in the recesses of your mind take on many forms; they never die, but they can get transferred to someone else or can lie dormant, waiting for someone to believe enough to take action. Dreams not lived can also frustrate your life by battling inside with your fears and procrastination. In this state you may tend to blame others for your lack of progression. But, strategically talking about your dreams is like adding water to displaced grass seed; it's the kiss of life that dreams need to prosper.

I know a woman who, as a child, loved reading the comic strips in the Sunday paper, and she dreamed of creating her own. She began drawing her characters and writing her storylines. It was the adventures of a young boy and his pals called "Sir Square Neck and His Friends." She never shared her concept for the story with anyone, and her enthusiasm to for writing and drawing her comic strip soon dimmed. She went on with her life of survival like most people.

Fast-forward about fifteen years, and here comes Sponge Bob Square Pants. Immediately the young lady recognized her dream being enjoyed by Stephen Hillenburg, the creator of the animated television series. She will never know the kind of success of the Sponge Bob creator because her dream was drawn on paper in private and was never shared with anyone.

Her telling this story now does her no good. Sir Square Neck and His Friends never came to life. The only positive thing about this story is that it can be a warning to you not to repeat her mistake. Water your dreams with words, and nurture them with activity. This is the mystery of dreaming: you never know how big a dream can become. All dreams begin in your mind and must transition out into the light. Words start a dream's growth.

As a young teenager, Joseph had a dream that he would rule over his family. In his excitement, he told his brothers. I do not have to tell you how that went. They tried to kill him and his dream, but his determination to fulfill his purpose and his faith in what God had revealed kept him going.

Joseph's brothers were most definitely haters. They took their hating beyond cruel words; they actually began plotting how to take him out. When they threw him in a pit, Joseph was like a weed growing in a gutter. They tried everything to get rid of him, but he had a dream to hold on to.

Haters know something you need to use: dreams rehearsed added with action and determination are destined to manifest. Haters are usually those closest to you: that coworker you eat lunch with, your best friend whose life is stagnated, your mother, father, sister, uncle, cousin—you get the point. Haters, unlike enemies, are not easy to detect to the untrained eye. But once identified can actually help you. Do the opposite of what they say.

You can't silence haters, but you can kill their influence. They don't want to hear your dreams, and you don't need to tell them your dreams. But practice rehearsing your dreams and adding a plan, and haters will either ignore you or start avoiding you. Either way, they can't hinder a believer.

There is nothing more dangerous than a dreamer with a pinch of faith. You do not need hundreds of resources to get started—just your faith and your obedience. That works every time. Dreams come true with much activity.

Remember the stray grass seed. It lived out its life just as green as the greenest grass in a well-manicured front yard. It does not matter where you start out, but how you end up. Dreams are for those with futures.

Ugly is defined as anything that is unpleasant to look at, anything that is not appealing. Ugly affects your emotions.

Some situations are very ugly. Ugliness in your life can hinder your progress as you try to seize your dream. But God loves operating in the impossible. The uglier the circumstances, the more power He must employ. And God is powerful enough to deal with anything ugly. You just have to engage your

DREAMSPIRATION

faith and move. You could be in the darkest of circumstances one day, and God will turn you 180 degrees the next day.

God loves turning things around. If you just look around, you will see and hear of everyday miracles. There's a story of young man in Atlanta who not only was the first African American male valedictorian in his high school in a decade but also was the recipient of one million dollars in scholarships. He had to brave negative peer pressure, the death of his brother, robbery at gunpoint, and his mother's fight with cancer. Yet he believed that God had a plan for his life, and he was determined to prove God right.

This young man received assistance from several organizations, including two Greek fraternities. He thanked them all in his speech on graduation day. There is no place for pride when you are trying to break out of where you are. Pride will keep you silent and stuck. Pride tells you that you do not need anybody to assist you. Ask for help while you are helping yourself.

When I see an ugly situation or circumstance, I get excited, because I know something great is about to happen. I do not create ugly and do not wish bad on anyone or anything. But let's face the facts: life happens. Ugly will always be here. What are you going to do about it?

According to the Bible, "Everything is beautiful in its time" (Ecclesiastes 3:11). That means that no matter how gritty the scenery, it will have its day in the sun. There will always be a light at the end of the tunnel. No matter how dire a situation, God's desire is for all to live prosperously. Everything has a time and season, but your function is to move toward the victory at every turn. Keep dreaming and desiring the good. That is the heart of a loving God.

"For I know the thoughts that I think toward you...thoughts of peace, and not evil to give you an expected end." - Jeremiah 29:11

Questions?

What kind of background do you have? How has it played a role in the pursuit of your dream?

Do you feel that your dream is too big or impossible? If so, why?

Have you spoken your dream aloud to yourself or someone you can trust? If not, why?

Are you embarrassed or afraid to talk about your dream with others? If so, why?

What kind of things lie in your gutter that may be stopping you from pursuing your dream?

WHY BE A HATER ?

4

"Hate is too great a burden to bear. It injures the hater more than it injures the hated."
— Coretta Scott King

Haters are not going away. They have been around since the dawn of time. The snake in the garden of Eden was a hater. The first recorded murder—Cain killed his brother, Abel—happened because Cain was a hater. The Pharisees and lawmakers hated on Jesus and plotted to crucify Him. We all have haters, and at times we have had moments where we hated on people, consciously and subconsciously.

Hatred is a painful state. If you are honest with yourself, you know that any time you criticize a dreamer, it does not make you feel better about yourself. And you know your position in life is out of place if you are numbered with the underachievers. Make this your last day as a hater. It is as easy as that! Ask yourself what hating gets you? Give others the right to dream so you do not hinder your own dreams.

Fear is one of the foundational hindrances to dreaming. What if you try something and it doesn't work? Well, what if it does? Either way you've lost nothing, but the opportunity for gain is greater. You can always go back.

Maximize this moment in your life. All you have is now. If you have reached middle age, you are literally on the countdown. What are you waiting for? Why are you sitting in the observer's seat, watching everyone else live while you criticize their boldness and bravery, and wait for them to fail? At least they're trying.

There was an inspirational e-mail going around a few years back that compared king Babe Ruth's home runs with his strikeouts. He had nearly twice as many strikeouts as home runs. If Babe Ruth had given up baseball after so many strikeouts, he would never have become a home run king.

Tony Braxton was told by a critic that she sounded like a man. That did not stop her from pursuing an eventually lucrative singing career and brought her several Grammies and a lengthy stint in Las Vegas. There are countless other stories of people who fought against the odds to be winners. Haters are not just haters, they are losers.

I have noticed something that all haters have in common: co-conspirators. They have to have someone to validate their thinking. Separating yourself from other haters will revolutionize your life. Two in agreement puts a seal on any mindset, positive or negative. It's the seed of the mob mentality.

Riots broke out across South Central Los Angeles in 1992 after the controversial Rodney King verdict, when four white and one Hispanic police officer were acquitted of using excessive force to subdue a black man after a traffic stop. Some of the rioters had never been in trouble with the law but agreed that the verdict was unjust and decided to take part. The mob mentality says that if that many people agree, it must be right, so let's follow them. The decision to destroy property and harm innocent people cost the city almost one billion dollars.

The point of the story is the force of unity. If you can get two people to agree with your cause, you can get one hundred. With that in mind, think of the connection between you and a dreamer, a mover, and a shaker. If a two-week riot can produce one billion dollars in damage, how much can two people accomplish when they agree to achieve something good?

When I was in high school, I did not get intimidated by the rumors of the gangs being drawn to Cobb County, Georgia where I attended school, or by the students who played the role of the local thugs. I hung with my boys. Intimidation was not part of my character, and we were a force to be reckoned with.

As I got older, my mind began to shift. Although I had not yet given my life to Christ, I had been taught right from wrong. I invited nearly fifty friends, male and female, over to my home for my father to talk to them about living in a positive light. These same friends started following me to church on Sundays.

One Friday night, my friends and I went to a revival, because we'd heard that there would be some "nice" young ladies there we could get with after the service. Our attention was zoned in on the girls, and we were not into what the

REFLECTIONS

ARE YOU A HATER?

Use this checklist to find out.

O I often say negative things about people.

O I find things to criticize about people.

O I believe people are jealous of me.

O I am right most of the time.

O I wait on people to fail.

O I enjoy seeing others fail.

O I enjoy proving people wrong or saying "I told you so."

O People do not often tell me their dreams or secrets.

O I rarely get excited about other people's accomplishments.

O I rarely give a sincere compliment to others.

O I talk behind people's backs and gossip.

O I agree with others when they say negative things.

O I do not get along well with other people, because everyone hates on me.

preacher was saying. But something he said caught my attention, and I looked up. At that moment I was called to the front of the church by the preacher so that he could pray for me. In an instant my life was forever changed. I accepted Christ, and within a couple of years, I got married and was promoted to be the youth pastor in my father's ministry.

Instead of hating, I was motivated to be just as influential or more than the leaders of the fledgling gangs in Cobb County. That was the seed form of Club VFL, the youth ministry of Victory Family Life Church, where my father was the pastor.

Being a hater has no rewards. All of its attributes are negative. You have to dislike what your peers are accomplishing through dreams. You have to ridicule them to their faces or talk with others who agree with your opinion. When you're a hater, you cannot move from where you are. So decide to be glad for those who are upwardly mobile. Cut yourself off from other haters, and make the choice to be among the winners.

There are great rewards in dreaming. God is calling all dreamers. Dreamers live in a dreamer's world. Despite what is going on around them, they live in the state of what they dream and talk about every day.

A man who wants to be a bodybuilder and dreams of being on the cover of Muscle Magazine cannot just go to work every day; eat hot dogs for lunch,; come home and sit in his recliner; pick up the phone to order a pizza; drink a beer while waiting for the pizza; turn on the NFL Network and watch the highlights from Sunday's game; eat pizza and drink another beer while watching Monday Night Football; and then finally nod off during the two-minute warning, content that his favorite team will hold its three-point lead. He then wakes up the next morning and starts all over again.

What happened to the dream of the picture on the cover? He needs to get some friends that encourage him to go for his dreams because they are aspiring bodybuilders or lawyers or principals, etc. who are going for theirs.

Haters and dreamers are like oil and water; they do not mix. Haters are stuck in life and have decided not to dream. Dreamers have a plan, and they check accomplishments off their list regularly. Dreamers ask for help and are helpers. Be conscious of the hater's ways, and refrain from doing the same things.

When you agree with labels haters use against you, you let go of your dreams. Change your conversation and change your life. When you start talking about your dreams and agreeing with those that dream, your atmosphere will go through a metamorphosis. You will look around for your former friends, and they will all be gone.

"Death and Life are in the power of the tongue; and they that love it shall eat its fruit." — Proverbs 18:21

Questions?

If you answered positively or agreed with any of the statements in the Reflections, start thinking about how you can change your negative patterns.

Are you happy for others when they achieve? Why, or why not?

Are you happy when others fail? Why, or why not?

Find ways to be happy for others when they succeed, knowing that if God can do it for them, He can do it for you.

YOU ARE NOT A VICTIM

5

"Never allow yourself to be made a victim. Accept no one's definition of your life, but define yourself."

— Harvey S. Firestone

Before you start collecting your opinion on what this chapter may be about, let me give a disclaimer. One definition of victim is a person who suffers from a destructive or injurious action or agency. You may have been the recipient of actions that you did not deserve. No one deserves to be victimized, but negative circumstances that you have no control over, are a part of living on this earth. Until you leave this earth, you will feel the pain of the consequences of what you have been through. You have to make a conscientious effort not to label yourself as a victim.

I know a middle-aged woman who has been making excuses for every unproductive area of her life. Because all the reasons point to someone else, she is powerless to do anything about her undesirable stations in life: her job, her standard of living, her health. Nothing is ever her fault; therefore, she never has to take responsibility for making a change. Since everything is beyond her control, she is sure to forever remain a victim of her circumstances. Her only success is in her ability to survive, and she has managed to do that for over thirty years.

You are called to do a lot more than survive. As a seed of Abraham (Galatians 3:27-29) you are called not only to thrive past your humble beginnings but to be a blessing to others. Romans 8:28 says that everything in your life is working together for your good as a chosen person and for God's purpose.

Everything you have been through—the good, the bad, and the ugly—has joined forces to give God glory and do you good.

If you have made up your mind to go full force in the direction of your dream, you have to resolve never to blame others for anything you can change. And have faith that God is going to handle the things you can't change. Maybe some awful things have happened to you; it does not matter. God guarantees you the victory in spite of any ugly that has tried to hinder you.

> *God, grant me the serenity to accept the things I cannot change, courage to change the things I can, and wisdom to know the difference.* — Reinhold Niebuhr

There are many examples in the Bible of people beating the odds and pushing past the most negative of circumstances: Daniel in the lion's den, the three Hebrew boys in the fiery furnace, etc. In the 2012 Olympics there was Oscar Pistorius who won the right to run in the 400 meter and 4 X 400 meter relay although a below-the-knee double amputee who runs using a prostheses. These victories were not just for them; it is also for you. You have to put your faith in action and live like a champion. The more time you spend blaming others, the less time you have to learn and practice ways of turning tragedies into triumphs. The reason you find yourself in certain calamities may be legitimate, but not legitimate enough to keep you down.

If you love the drama and the attention being down brings, you can count on never being successful. Only people with the mental tenacity to do some work will move beyond mediocre lifestyles. You should want to be more than average. Striving for a C grade when an A is available to all does not make sense. Reach for the stars; you just might grab hold of one.

One day a substitute teacher and I found ourselves in a conversation about dropping seeds of wisdom everywhere we go. She told me how sometimes she finds herself in a discussion with students who insist on blaming their teachers for their bad grades. She had told them that all students start out with an A on the first day of school. The only way to keep an A is to follow the criteria that is given at the beginning of the school year. A syllabus is often given out for all students to follow so they can succeed. Teachers are glad when students look for ways to pass. If a midterm exam counts for 25 percent of the grade and a student achieves a 50 percent, he or she can count on an 88 percent if all other criteria are met. With extra credit, it is still possible for that student to get an A. One bad grade does not make a failing student. A class where 75 percent of the students are failing gives the teacher a bad reputation.

It's the same principle in life. God does not want anyone to fail. It is His desire for all to do well and to achieve their measure of success. In class, some students may not be a good test taker but may excel in homework, reports, and class participation. Their test-taking skills may be their handicap.

God specializes in handicaps. He gets the glory. He took advantage of the fact that Lazarus had been dead for four days before Jesus came to see about his friend (John 11:14). There was a belief among the Jewish people that a person could return to life a few days after dying. They had witnessed it before. But four days was out of the question. To prove God had power over traditional thinking, Jesus waited before heading back after hearing about Lazarus's sickness.

Line your life up with the fact that it is God's desire to see you thrive. You may have been victimized, but you are not a victim. Victims hold on to the mindset that they can always expect bad things to happen to them. And it becomes a self-fulfilling prophecy. It rotates around and around. Every victory must have a dungeon for them to fall into, so victims look for the dungeon. When victims find themselves in a dry place, they assume they are cursed as usual. They believe they are destined for failure like always.

You know if this is you; you know if you've been a victim. Stop making excuses, and do something to make your life better. There is always a way of

DREAMSPIRATION

Nelson Mandela was a great dreamer and visionary. This South African leader was sent to prison in 1963 on charges of trying to sabotage the government, which advocated a policy called apartheid that treated people of different races differently. (Mandela advocated for a democratic society in which all people would be treated equally.) Mandela spent the next twenty-seven years in prison.

But after he was released in 1990, he forgave the people who had imprisoned him. He could have come out of prison hateful, angry, and ready for revenge—wanting to somehow reclaim the years that were taken away from his family. Instead, he refused to let hatred and unforgiveness consume him and distract him from his purpose—a dream that was bigger than him.

Mandela's dream would help to transform an entire nation. He became South Africa's first black president and delivered speeches internationally in which he urged people to forgive each other because forgiveness is God's plan and therefore always the right thing to do.

escape for every temptation. It is a sin not to believe what God says about you (Romans 14:23). You must always remember to act in faith. Walk in faith, and trust the God in you.

It does not matter how God chooses to bless you; He wants you to do well. He is going to take care of you by any means necessary. Embrace the opportunities that God sends your way; don't be too proud to accept His way. He is not going to direct you to sin or to do others wrong.

When you are blessed and prospering, you will be living your dream, and you will have to tell the story of how you arrived there, because it will not be obvious to others. Do not reject this personal testimony—your personal story. No one knows like you do how you made it.

The bad things that happened to you did happen, but they are not happening now. Your testimony is grand because you have a handicap. It keeps you humble when you "arrive," and it gives others hope.

REFLECTIONS

HOLDING ON TO HURT?

Use this checklist to find out.

○ Has someone hurt you in the past, and you are still holding on to that hurt?

○ Is there someone in your past, dead or alive, that you have not forgiven for hurting you?

○ When you deal with difficult situations that are out of your control, do you feel resentful and angry because of the outcome?

○ When you feel bad, do you try to make others feel bad, guilty, or sorry for you?

○ Do you blame others easily when something goes wrong?

○ Do you have a hard time accepting your responsibility for your bad choices?

○ Do you feel that people owe you something because of what you've gone through?

There is always a way that leads to winning, and it is your job to seek it out. Roadblocks point you in the direction designed for you, so don't think like a victim. Chasing after the wind is a losing battle. You cannot change what happened to you, but you can plan a new direction for your life. Just stop and ask for help. "Lord, which way do you want me to go?" He is waiting for you to ask. "The steps of a good man are ordered by the Lord" (Psalms 37:23-24).

You are not going to be rescued from your current life. You have already been rescued, and a door has been opened for you (Revelation 3:8). Jesus came to give you life—not just any old life, but a life of abundance. You are called to be blessed and to be a blessing. All you have to do is walk in it.

Dreamers are not victims. They do not have time to grumble and complain. They have work to do. It is time for you to get to work. And the hardest job for you is to think past your doubt. When that becomes habit, nothing will be kept back. Go after your dreams with your whole heart; God is eager to manifest them in your life.

Think about it this way: Since God loves showing up in your weakness, you are going to walk around with plenty of power, even though you have handicaps. God gets the glory in your weakness. God infuses you with strength if you admit that you need His help. Do not fall prey to the world system of supporting you as a victim so you continually need others' resources. You are more than a conqueror because God loves you and has a better plan for you.

Yes, you were a victim, but that was in the past. Now you have been made new and given the opportunity to pursue your passion. You have the authority to go further than you have ever imagined. Use your testimony as your guide. Always be ready to give an account of how you arrived at the new you. You are victorious.

Questions?

If you answered yes to any of the Reflections questions, how can you change your thinking?

What is your plan for walking in forgiveness, joy, and positivity?

If you answered no to all of the questions, how do you deal with people who display these traits?

FRIENDS

6

"Things change. And friends leave. Life doesn't stop for anybody."
— Stephen Chbosky

Not all of your friends will want to go with you when you decide to leave the place you are in. There are many reasons for this, and I will try to ease your burden by explaining the problem.

Your due time may not coincide with that of everyone you are around. When you hear your higher calling, you must follow it. There may be a time of loneliness, but God knows where He has you. Stay close to His voice, and He will direct you. There is nothing lonely about the kingdom of God. If you keep moving forward, you will run into others going your way. You will find you have more fulfilling relationships than you ever had. You will relate better to those who speak what you speak. You will wonder why you didn't look for this place sooner.

At this point in your dreaming, you may feel a desire to go back and get those left behind—and some may come looking for you. It is really overwhelming when you spend many days and months reaching out to old connections only to find they do not want to follow you. This is what casting your pearls to swine means. Jesus said, "Do not give dogs what is sacred; do not throw your pearls to pigs. If you do, they may trample them under their feet, and then turn and tear you to pieces" (Matthew 7:6).

Pigs live in a pen filled with mud. They eat there too. In their law, Jews are not allowed to eat swine. When Jesus gave his Sermon on the Mount to a great crowd of Jews, He made this point: After you are delivered from something, you can attempt to bring others to where you are. But do not waste your time. If they resist, then stop trying. It would be like putting pearls in a pig trough. These same people you are trying to help will turn around and criticize you.

It is not easy to watch friends stay back in the same circumstances you worked so hard to escape. But if they believe you now think you are better than them, their pride may not allow them to receive your words. You would be fighting a losing battle if you attempt to pressure them into changing. When you encourage them, testify to them, and argue with them, yet they do not change, you have wasted time and probably lost their friendship.

The best way to handle these times is to simply tell them what has happened for you and to be available if they want advice. Your changed life is more of an inspiration than all the words you can ever say. Everyone is not ready for change, and each person responds to change differently. Some people embrace it, while others run from it. If you are giving unsolicited counsel, some friends may perceive your encouragement as bragging. You do not stop loving them; you just can't help them right now.

Then there are friends who do follow you, but refuse to change. You may wonder why they are here. They can see what is happening for you, and they follow the excitement, but are not looking for their own; they want your crumbs. They have no desire for change, but they are glad you changed. These friends turn into acquaintances. You let them ride, but you do not entangle yourself with their struggles. It's like having distant relatives. They are still related, but they have no influence over you.

Do not despair; old friends are sometimes your biggest supporters. Having friends is a powerful gift. A true friend loves you at all times. They will be like a brother or sister to you in any adversity. No matter where you find yourself, a true friend is invaluable. I remember being told as a child about choosing good friends. I found out a person's possessions or status in life does not guarantee they will make a good friend. Neither will a person just because he or she is a neighbor.

A good friend is similar to a good spouse; the relationship can whether any storm. The storms are what prove the bond. If a relationship is based on truth, it is an honest one. When a friend has an ulterior motive for the friendship, it will be revealed when things do not go as planned. You know who your true friends are, because they can handle troubled waters.

Oasis Family Life Church members are a close-knit congregation. We thrived for months when we first started in a high school cafeteria. I could not imagine the church would move and leave any of its members behind. But believe it or not, there were some who said that we were doing good right where we were. They wanted to stay.

Needless to say, everyone did not move to the new building. This scenario is inevitable when you make a decision to move vigorously in the direction of a dream. All of your friends and associates cannot go. Some will not want to go, and others will go, but they will not change. As you progress, some will leave, and you will gain new.

There is an old saying that says friends come into your life for a reason, a season, or a lifetime. The lifetime friends grow in your direction. These are the keepers. These relationships are mutually beneficial.

Stay away from something called survivor's guilt. This is a state in which you struggle with your own progress. You succumb to the foolishness of thinking of yourself as a traitor. All your old friends are surviving without change. You go back and visit, and there they sit. They aren't doing much better than when they graduated high school, and it is twenty years later.

You should not brag or gossip about old friends. Live your life, reach out, and help the ones that want it. Joseph's destiny (found in the book Genesis) propelled him to save a nation. His dreams took him to the top of his game. Had he not dreamed, an entire generation of people would have been lost.

See yourself as a chosen one. Accept the challenge to be the leader among many. There are friends for you at each level. Embrace your change, and let God lead you to your prepared destiny.

Some of you never dream in your own world but fantasize about the life of others, based on what you can see. But you do not know what it took for them to achieve their dreams. Runners have to condition themselves for months and even years before they can win a long-distance race. Their bodies, minds, and hearts cooperate with each other to ensure they have the endurance to make it to the end. Of course, each runner would love to win, but in the end, only one person wins.

What makes runners try again and again, knowing their odds aren't good? For them the joy and success comes in finishing the race. People who are in good physical shape but have not trained rigorously can try to win a long-distance race—and may even finish. But they feel that the pain and fatigue was not worth it. Their attitude becomes negative, because they went after the results without being prepared.

This is what happens to you when we chase after a dream with the wrong motive; you burn out, get frustrated, and quit easily. People's lives prepare them for the ability to achieve their dreams not the dreams of others.

Be You: Stop Identity Theft!

Stories abound about identity theft. It is the latest in white-collar crime. You hear about it on the news, and you read about it in the paper. Someone's Social Security number is compromised, and the impersonation is on. The person's credit is used, and her reputation is smeared. This fiasco takes years to repair. Hundreds of companies have been created to help stem the tide of this latest crime wave.

I have yet to hear about remedies for helping people committing this crime. Where are they going to get help? You know that one of the purposes for jail is to rehabilitate the offender. Hopefully the identity thieves that get caught can have a change of heart after spending some time behind bars. But, where is the help for the people that are simply copy cats. They never developed their own passion or stuck with any of their desires long enough to make it successful.

These thieves do not understand the grace it takes to grow into being who God has called them to be. Do you know what God's grace is? Merriam-Webster's dictionary defines *grace* as,

- unmerited divine assistance given humans for their regeneration and sanctification;
- a special favor;
- a temporary exemption; or
- approval or favor.

Never take the grace extended to you or others for granted. You may not have the same grace extended to you as someone else. That is why we should always stay in the will of God. When you step outside of God's will, you open yourself up to dangers and consequences you may not be able to bear. It is fine to go after a dream, but be sure it is your own dream—the dream God has placed in your heart to help fulfill your purpose.

• •

God's grace is individual. He delivers a specific dosage of grace to you when you are in His will. Even some of the things you see as negative or bad increase your endurance and your will to keep running. In the moments when you want to quit or when something gets in your way God steps in with His grace. He gives the extra wind you need to keep going, because you are determined to finish. And despite what you've been through, you still get excited and joyful at the thought of achieving your dream.

If your attitude begins to change, it is a great time to make sure you're on the right track. It's normal to feel tired, frustrated, or overwhelmed sometimes when you are going after your dream. But the conditioning of your mind and heart should keep you joyful. If you begin to feel resentful, bitter, angry—and even if the thought of achieving your dream no longer brings you joy—begin to seek God through prayer and reading His Word. This will reconnect you with your true purpose and dreams so you can get back on track.

When you chase someone else's dreams, you often find or connect with your true purpose along the way. Denying yourself the opportunity to explore these feelings is what can sometimes cause you to feel inner turmoil—a pull or tug in your subconscious that tells you that you are going the wrong way. Something triggers you, and you are left with a difficult decision. And until you make the right decision, that feeling keeps resurfacing.

This is why many people with seemingly wonderful careers suddenly quit and pursue something unexpected. Doctors leave million-dollar practices to go

REFLECTIONS

ARE YOU AN IDENTITY THIEF ?

O Do you look at others' lives and wish you have what they have?

O Do you act outside of your "normal" when you are around a particular person or group of people?

O Do you feel resentful, bitter, or angry, even though you are pursuing your goals?

O Do you have secret hobbies or passions that no one around you knows about, because they don't fit in with what people around you are doing?

O Do you love your hobby, talent, or volunteer work more than your career?

O Do you have someone that you want to be like, and you find yourself acting, dressing, or talking like them?

O Do you idolize a friend, family member, celebrity, public figure, co-worker, acquaintance, or peer?

O Are you struggling to hold on to an image that you feel doesn't portray who you are anymore?

live in huts in a third world country so they can deliver help to people in need. A lawyer, John Grisham, left a thriving career in law to become a fiction writer, and his books ended up on the best-seller list time and time again.

Do not get stuck living someone else's dream—stealing someone else's identity. Make sure you are always connected to the will of God. There are times when you may be nudged to go in a different direction than you planned, but it's not for you to chase someone else's dream or to try to live someone else's life with the wrong motives and lack of preparation. If you are nudged in a different direction, it should only be in a deeper pursuit of your own dreams.

There is a principle in psychology: "association brings about assimilation." You have to watch who you are hanging with. Either they will be influencing you or you will be influencing them. This is just how the mind works. That's why God's Word speaks of such things as assembling with other believers and not being influenced by unbelievers.

Whether you choose to believe this or not is inconsequential. Listen to your conversations with certain people. Is this how you used to talk when you were not keeping company with them? What dreams did you used to have before you started entertaining these new friends?

I implore you to flip the script and change your company. Step out and dare to be different. Be the first one in your family to do something to the extreme. You know you have been dreaming about it. God specializes in the impossible, so all you have to do is believe and take action. Help will appear from some unlikely places.

You have probably heard the expression "When the student is ready, the teacher will come," but here is another one: "When the dreamer acts, miracles respond." Miracles are reserved for those who dare to believe.

Live out your own identity. The red carpet is only for real stars. Copycats and fairytale chasers do not get to walk on it. Create your own red carpet affair. What inspires you? You would not be dreaming if the power of the almighty God could not give the dream life through you. To really climb the ladder of your own success, be yourself. Stop committing identity theft.

"My grace is sufficient for you, for my strength is made perfect in weakness."
                                                            — 2 Corinthians 12:9

Questions?

If you answered yes to any of the Reflections questions, you may be in an identity struggle. It's time to get to know you. You are beautifully and wonderfully made.

Are there friends in your circle that you need to keep away from? Make a plan for how you will achieve this.

Do you feel guilty for going after your dreams? Why?

Do you really want to find out who you are and to connect with your purpose? What sacrifices can you make to achieve this goal?

How can you make a step toward revealing your true self to others?

If you are committed to finding out who you are, write down three things that you genuinely and truly enjoy and love, no matter how strange, silly, different, or unique you may think they are. Share these things with at least one trusted person.

If these questions do not apply to you, do you know someone who is pretending to be something they are not? How can you make it easier for that person to be himself or herself?

METAMORPHOSIS NEEDED

7

"Be the change that you wish to see in the world."

— Mahatma Gandhl

You have dreamed of doing great things. You started, but keep finding yourself right back where you began. You cannot figure out what the problem is. You have talked to people and sat down with leaders known for their wisdom. You make a valiant effort again and again—the second, third, fourth, and fifth time. Getting over the same hurdle seems like a never-ending battle.

Have you ever thought about the fact that you keep starting and continuing with the same you? Changing your surroundings does not guarantee a change unless you change you. You need a metamorphosis.

The word metamorphosis is derived from a Greek word meaning "transformation." If you stay just like you are and add education, career, and all the decorations of life, you will still be discontent if you never change you. You take you with you. A cycle of small victories back to struggle is the way you are destined to live without a complete change of heart.

Why does a millionaire football player get arrested and charged with drug trafficking? Why does the educated, gainfully employed couple living in an upper-middle-class neighborhood constantly borrow to pay their mortgage and are regularly threatened with repossession of their vehicles? A metamorphosis is needed.

DREAMSPIRATION

Brenda worked as an accountant at a Fortune 500 corporation. But she regularly found herself fighting to make ends meet and battling depression. She eventually moved back in with her mother.

Brenda and her three siblings were raised in a single-parent home. Her mother, Carol, was a server at chain restaurants. Carol made the decision early that she would not get stuck in the welfare system like so many of her coworkers and neighbors. Carol decided to use her natural beauty and womanly wows to supplement her income; she solicited the company of many "uncles," who frequented her bedroom. She skillfully decorated her tiny apartment and kept her children clean and dressed with thrift-store fashions. And all the men bought into her scheme. After she fed and took good care of them in her bed, she quietly requested assistance with her bills.

As a young girl and the eldest child, Brenda watched the parade of shame throughout her childhood, teenage, and young adult years. As an above-average student, her young life showed promise. With the assistance of her favorite English teacher, she applied to several colleges and was accepted to the local state university.

Brenda had made the choice as a young girl that she would never live as her mother did. She would get an education and make a better life for herself. She made a conscious effort not to get pregnant without having a husband and not to raise her children in poor circumstances.

After high school, Brenda went to college and majored in accounting. During her senior year, she was offered an internship as an accountant's assistant in the company that would later hire her on permanently.

Brenda graduated on time and was hired, as promised, by the accounting firm. While still living with her mom, she met and married a man she was introduced to at her local gym. All seemed to be going well. She had started out in her new career with a midrange income. And her husband, a school bus driver and handyman, was caring and supportive. They moved into a gated community, and in three years she had three children.

But Brenda's attitude began to change. The finances were a little tight, and she began pressuring her husband to get a better job or an additional one. The household started to fall apart. You could frequently find the children in their bedroom crying and upset after they witnessed a loud argument between their parents.

When Brenda could have been taking classes to obtain her master's and become a CPA, she was estranged from her husband and entangled in a distressing divorce. She struggled to keep some normalcy in the children's lives and to pay all the mounting bills.

The marriage finally ended, and Brenda worked as much overtime as she could to maintain her independence. She just could not seem to get a hold of what was happening to her life. Her dream of successful living—void of the problems she had grown up with—had faded into oblivion. After a year of moving twice, fighting to stay in the same school district, she asked her mom if she and the kids could move in temporarily.

Brenda soon found that her mother's lifestyle had not changed. Not only did Carol entertain several different men, she encouraged her daughter to do the same. This troublesome environment was too much for Brenda. It pushed her deeper into a retreat from life. She worked dutifully at the firm and came home to her darkened bedroom, where she slept without television or even knowing the whereabouts of her young family. She had no thought of whether they were eating, doing their homework, or being looked after.

It was ironic that this is exactly how Brenda, herself, had been raised. Her mother would work odd hours, and when she was at home, she filled her time with bedroom entertainment and late-night dating.

Nicole had watched Brenda at work over the years and had seen firsthand the decline in Brenda. During lunch one day she decided to invite Brenda to her church, just to get her out of the house. She could see that Brenda needed some help. Brenda began attending Nicole's church along with her three children. Brenda made friends with other people her age who were positive and supportive. As she began to open up about her life, she found out she could get budgeting help through the church.

As requested, Brenda brought all her bills with her to her first session. She had no idea that she would find the enlightenment she so desired. As the budgeting minister sat down with her and her bills, she began to ask Brenda how she came to be in her current predicament. Brenda began to explain the last decade of her life and the fact that she now felt stuck.

Brenda had made an intelligent choice not to continue to live in poverty, but she had gone off into life with no vision better than her mother's. Her mother did not want the stereotype of a system-supported single parent, and Brenda did not want to depend on men to take care

DREAMSPIRATION

of her and her children. Where was the plan? Brenda's mother decided that men were her way out, and Brenda decided that a college degree would get her out.

First of all, men are human and therefore fallible, and you can't put your trust in things that are fallible. Second, any life coach will tell you that a college degree is not a bad thing, but a college degree cannot change your way of thinking if you don't know it needs to change. In fact, you can be successful even without a college degree. Living life standing on a sure foundation is the only way not to stay down when you fall.

Brenda's story ended well. She had no clue that she was repeating what she had learned as a child: the art of escaping success and proper planning. After analyzing her budget, it was discovered that she could maintain in her own apartment and have money left to save. Her dreams, which were not based on proven strategies, had soon turned into a nightmare, because she did not have the knowledge to plan and had not been exposed to new ways of thinking.

Brenda's metamorphosis did not include criticizing her mother, but bringing her life into harmony with the established rules of order. She already had the fixings to be great in her field. All she needed was a complete transformation in her mindset. Her first step was to forgive her past and her mother, so that she could start with a clean slate into the life that was designed specifically for her.

You may have said that you will never live like other family members. But that alone is not strong enough to give you the change that will keep history from repeating itself. Living by principles is the only foolproof solution. The biblical principles that govern life are 100 percent guaranteed to work.

Just because you set yourself up as better than what you witnessed growing up does not draw power to help you to change. You have to study what was missing from what you experienced. The answer will always come back as the absence of certain principles. If you decided to do it "your own way," I can tell you that you will find yourself repeating what you most hate.

To reconcile your way of thinking with God's plan for your life, you need a total metamorphosis. A caterpillar will never turn into a butterfly without first creating and remaining in its pupa. A butterfly's life cycle consists of four stages: egg, larva (the caterpillar stage), pupa (resting stage), and finally adult (beautiful butterfly).

Change is a process. Saying you want to be successful one day does not turn you into a success the next. Second Corinthians 5:17 says it like this: "If anyone is in Christ Jesus old things are passed away, behold all things become new." Become in its simplest form is "come to be." You have to come into your change.

In the 1983 movie Trading Places, actor Eddie Murphy is a streetwise hustler who is kidnapped to take the place of an up-and-coming financial tycoon in an irreverent experiment that explores how surroundings can change character.

Dressed in expensive threads, Murphy's character begins to steal the exquisite trappings in "his" mansion. As he stuffs golden candleholders and cigarette lighters into his jacket pockets, his butler constantly reminds him that he doesn't need to steal those things, because they're his. Then he has a party and invites all his friends from the ghetto to his new house. After taking note that they have no respect for his nice things, he begins to kick them all out.

Change is not an overnight process. You have to become new. The Bible does not say you are new, but that you become new. You end up with the same person that God originally intended for you to be.

Caterpillars and matured butterflies are all same. The caterpillar is the larva stage of the beautiful butterfly. Many people reject larva as ugly, but that is only one stage as they develop into their destiny. You may be in your ugly state right now. But you are not going to stay ugly. But your transformation from ugly to fine is up to you; it takes work.

A larva is a voracious eater; it eats and eats as it grows up to two inches. After this stage, it finds a safe place to become a pupa. It creates a sack out of saliva and leaves, and it stays in that sack for up to two weeks. During this time, it eats nothing, just like a bear in hibernation.

Before God took Oasis Family Life Church to where it is now, I went through a pupa state many times over. After going through a personal home foreclosure, I found myself, along with my wife and two daughters, living with my brother and his family. I knew that this stage was not permanent, so I suffered through it until my next stage came. I continued dreaming and thriving, and ministry continued; we did not miss a beat. I knew, beyond any doubt or haters, that all this was working together for my future good. The proof is in what God has done for Oasis Family Life Church and me personally since my transformation.

Never be afraid to change. A caterpillar has to leave the comfort of the warm grass and abundance of food to subside in a cocoon for two weeks before it reaches its destiny. You have to know that you were born for more.

Do not sweat the down times; they are preparing you for what you are dreaming of. The larva wills itself to suffer, separated from the rest of creation.

Without the cocoon, it has no chance of survival. So into the pupa it goes until a metamorphosis takes place. Then, while it is still warm, a beautiful butterfly bursts onto the scene.

When you are going toward your dreams, nothing can hinder your progress but you. Get yourself out of the way, and learn a new way. Why would you want to hold onto something that has not worked in twenty-five years? Living by principles that have already proven successful is the smartest direction to travel.

It is time for your metamorphosis. Start today with the decision to begin your walk into your change. As you do, remember you are no longer a caterpillar. You can no longer hang with caterpillars, because they cannot fly. You are soaring now. Imagine a beautiful butterfly crawling around with caterpillars with his powdery rainbow wings dragging on the ground. That's just ridiculous. Get up and stay up, you are now a butterfly.

Questions?

What stage of metamorphosis are you in: egg, caterpillar, cocoon, or butterfly? Why?

How long have you been in your current stage?

Are you ready to go to the next stage? If so, what do you need to get you to the next stage?

PART 2

Dream Big,
Dream Bigger

ANACONDA DREAMING

8

"God gives us dreams a size too big so that we can grow into them."

— Unknown

After you've changed your thinking and your environment to be more conducive to accomplishing your dream and have taken steps toward defining yourself and your goals, it's time to take the next step and dream big.

An associate of mine has a keen interest in the animal world. At one point he had a snake. One day he said that anacondas grow in proportion to their environment. Bam! I had a great analogy for dreaming big. To dream big, you have to be in the right place.

If you want to expand your dream, you have to move your mind (or in some cases your person) to a place that is conducive to growth. You should hang around people who will challenge you intellectually. So add some highly successful people to your lunch rotation.

When I began this book, I knew that I would share facts backed by statistics. After beginning to research my associate's statement about anacondas, I became frustrated. I could find no data that proved that anyone could manipulate the growth of a snake. About forty minutes into my search, I ran across a young man's inquiry on a snake website. He wanted to know if he could buy an anaconda and limit how big it grew.

Anacondas grow to be the heaviest snakes in the world. According to the site ExtremeScience.com the largest anaconda ever measured was twenty-eight feet long, forty-four inches wide, and about 162 pounds. There have been unsubstantiated sightings in South America of anacondas up to fifty feet long. Currently, a national museum of wildlife is offering a fifty-thousand-dollar reward for the capture and donation of an anaconda of this size.

Anacondas are known for their skittishness and their ability to squeeze the life out of a large animal. Their size and temperament makes them intriguing to people, including the young man on the Internet who asked if there is a way to stop the snake from growing to such an enormous size.

Before the scientist on the site answered the young man's question he recommended that the young man get a smaller species of snake. And then he said that a snake's growth could be stunted by putting it in a smaller cage. He ended his long response with some powerful food for thought. You can stunt an anaconda's growth, but it is a form of abuse. A small cage is not a healthy environment: it will also stunt the snake's life span.

You do not want to be numbered with those who purposely stunt the growth of a dream. A dream cannot flourish in your fears. Take your dream out of its small cage and put it on the stage where it belongs. Let it grow as large as it can get. Share your dream, live in your dream and prosper in it. Once put in the right environment you cannot stop its growth.

DREAMSPIRATION

Vivien Thomas was an African American surgical technician who developed the procedures used to treat blue baby syndrome in the 1940s. He was an assistant to surgeon Alfred Blalock in Blalock's experimental animal laboratory at Vanderbilt University in Nashville and later at the Johns Hopkins University in Baltimore, Maryland. Without an education past high school, Thomas rose above poverty and racism to become a cardiac surgery pioneer and a teacher of operative techniques to many of the country's most prominent surgeons. He was the first African American without a doctorate to perform open heart surgery on a white patient in the United States.

Thomas had a purpose and dream that was so big that any person alive during that time would have said it was impossible. But instead of living in fear and doubt, Thomas embraced his purpose and did something with his life that saved millions.

If you know anything about pregnancy, you know the last trimester can be a very trying time. Many women experience frustration, irritation, and impatience. The season of incubation is almost over, but the dream has yet to manifest. It is now the thirty-sixth week, and the baby must be born. It cannot stay in the womb much longer. Staying longer will threaten the life of the baby and the mother.

A close relative of mine became fearful on the day of her delivery. In the pangs of labor, she asked if maybe she could wait until tomorrow. Thank God that she did not have the power to make that happen. She was many centimeters dilated, and her cervix was fully effaced—meaning it was time. When the time comes, the baby's system is changing to adapt to the world outside the womb.

So it is with your dreams; you must allow them to grow outside of your mind. Your dreams are a part of who you are until they are birthed. Outside of you, they are bigger than you. When you do not bring them into the light of day and nourish them with the opportunity to expand, you are neglecting the very heart of what God is expecting of you.

An average anaconda is supposed to grow from eleven to twenty feet long. It should live ten to twelve years in the wild—but up to twenty years in captivity because of a steady diet and better health. What does that say about your dreams? You are supposed to take your dreams captive and focus them in your imagination. Make plans for them and showcase them. They grow only when exposed to the light of your faith. Talk about them with the right people, and ask for help with them. Let your small dreams grow.

• •

Carl Bradley was an up-and-coming minister in a medium-sized congregation. The congregation's pastor, Dr. Rower, was active in his New York community. In his evangelical work, he came across a young team of Asian nationals who had formed a Christian fellowship. They were diligently seeking someone to pastor their group, and they needed a place to gather.

After some consideration, Dr. Rower decided that Minister Bradley would lead the service for the fellowship. They would gather in one of the classrooms during Sunday school.

The gathering proved to be a very successful endeavor. The Asian congregation grew, and Minister Bradley learned some new things to add to the worship service. They soon had to move to a larger classroom.

Minister Bradley asked his pastor for an assistant to help him serve communion. Dr. Rower sent another young minister, Kevin Caldwell. Minister Caldwell and Minister Bradley worked well together at first. But Minister Caldwell began to complain to Dr. Rower regularly about Minister Bradley. He did not like the way he began service; he did not like the way he conducted offering; and he thought the altar prayer was too long. Whenever anything was different from the way he would do it, he would run and tell.

After several meetings with Minister Bradley, Dr. Rower realized that the problem was not with Minister Bradley but with Minister Caldwell. Dr. Rower, also a licensed psychologist, decided to set up a counseling session with the young minister.

At first glance, it seemed that Minister Caldwell was jealous of Minister Bradley's leadership status. Twenty minutes into the session, his countenance began to change. There was evidently something going on with him that had nothing to do with the Asian ministry.

Dr. Rower began to inquire about Kevin's personal life. He asked the young man about his dreams and aspirations. Suddenly, a bombshell of a dream started to unfold. As a single man and a committed sanctuary server, Kevin had dreamed for years of being a missionary worker in a poor country in Africa. The pastor was overjoyed that his young minister was not a disgruntled worker after all, but a man afraid of his seemingly gigantic desires.

What transpired was months of planning and of assembling several other members and community leaders who had felt compelled by the same dream. This started an African outreach ministry from this medium-sized congregation that not only impacted the lives of the American delegation but also the many lives in a small African country.

• •

What Minister Caldwell did, you may have done: sat on a dream that seemed overwhelming. You are too afraid to share it or so full of doubt that you know that it cannot be for you. When not acted on, dreams become a source of aggravation and frustration.

An old copy of a Random House Dictionary says that the words ignore and ignorance come from the Latin ignorare, which means to not know or to disregard. When you ignore your dreams, you are actually acting in ignorance; you do not know what can happen if you step out on faith and reach for them. You have nothing to lose by seeking and asking—except your own ignorance.

Once you do research on your dream, you may find that you are not the only one who has started from where you are. This is the Information Age, after all, and there is so much information right at your fingertips. Yet you have to be selective and make sure that your information is from a reputable source.

Do not keep your dreams locked up where they can never become real.

Your dream should not be just a fantasy. The word fantasy has several definitions. The one that describes anaconda dreaming is "unrestrained imagination." The only hope for your mind is to stick with the principles embedded in your heart by the Lord. God is so much bigger than what your mind can conceive. Allow Him to lead you to the place prepared just for you.

Move out of your little corner in your little house. Open up your mind to new horizons. It is time for you to get a bigger cage. Be the anaconda that wants to grow to twenty feet and live twenty years. Do not allow yourself to stay ignorant. Start today on your journey to fulfilling the desire put in your heart by God.

Questions?

Do you have a big dream to achieve, or a small dream to achieve in a big way? Write it down and tell someone.

How can you remove the limits from your dreams?

How will your dream help others?

YOU CAN ALWAYS STAY WHERE YOU ARE

9

"If what you're doing is not your passion, you have nothing to lose."
— Unknown

You have nothing to lose. You have heard this before; probably more than a few times. But today I want to ingrain it in your brain so much that you get up tomorrow morning saying, "Today I'm going to go for something I've always dreamed about but never had the nerve to try, because I have nothing to lose."

Why not try for the top every time out? You may have never asked yourself that question. The way you live has become habit. You have been in the clerical field for four years, and you want a promotion, so you apply for a receptionist job. I'm not knocking the receptionist position, but do you really want that after four years of typing, filing, and answering the phones? In honesty, most would say, "No!"

What do you really have to lose by going for the top? I do not believe in average, so I have to go for the top. I can always stay where I am, but it will not be because I did not try to move up. Back in the day when I was dating, I wanted the fine girls. I said, "I'm fine, so why do I want less than me." Now, stop right there. You better be agreeing with me about yourself. You have to know you are fine too. If you are one hundred pounds overweight, you better be looking good. Be the best-looking two tons of fun. If you do not think like that of yourself, no one else will either.

I go for the top. That's why I married the top. I will not settle; I refuse to settle for less. I have the same opportunity the so-called successful people have. I dare to try, even if I do not get what I am going after. It is better to try and fail than to not have tried at all.

I was a barber by trade. And I was the best. At fifteen, my Saturdays were jumping. At seventeen, I had my own car and insurance. I just always believed in trying. When I got the urge for pastoring, I went out and started from nothing, knowing that I would not stay there. Why not push toward the top? What's wrong with the dream of a megachurch?

To get it, I have to have the mindset that would propel me to the top. The "Mom and Pop" corner store mentality will not work. I can't know all of my customers by name. I may not know how everyone looks. Do you think the mayor of Atlanta knows everyone in his community by name? You think he knows Sharon Boyd had a ten-pound baby girl last week?

Maynard Jackson was the mayor of Atlanta for twelve years (serving eight of those consecutively). He was the first African American mayor ever in the history of the United States. He was so good, the people he served voted him mayor in 1973 and reelected him in 1977. Legally, he could not run for a third consecutive term. He knew his power in the Atlanta community and ran again in 1989, winning with 79 percent of the vote. One of the losing candidate's political strategists put it this way: "Maynard Jackson is god in this town, and you can't beat God."

I say the same to you; you can't beat God. With God on your side, you have to try for something way beyond your means. If God did not make Oasis Family Life Church a mega ministry, then it wouldn't have happened. But it would not have been because I did not give it every effort. I do not believe that it will phase out to nothing but either way I can always go back to cutting hair! Decide to try. You really have nothing to lose.

Carol Kent was a school bus driver. She heard her pastor say in one of his sermons that everyone should go after something they do not qualify for. She asked herself, Why not? She could always continue to drive school buses for minimum wage in conjunction with getting those school trips for extra money.

Carol lived in the south, but she applied online for an administrative job in Washington, D.C. The job paid four times more than she was making as a driver. In a week she was called for an interview over the phone, and she got the job. She knows it was her faith in action because she had never made that much money nor had she worked in the government sector as a civilian. There would be a lot she would have to learn, but she was willing, because she owed it to herself and

God, who gave her the opportunity.

What do you really have to lose? Are you afraid to fail? Who is grading you? This is not a test to see if you are going to the next grade. I remember those state tests; the administration struck fear in my heart about taking them. Come prepared, get a good night's rest, bring two pencils, you will have to be quiet, eat a good breakfast... Thankfully, you do not have to do all of that. All you have to do is adjust your attitude until you know that anything is possible if you believe. Then add some action to your belief. Some people say they believe, but there dream stays in their head. Yeah, it keeps them going, but it never does their life any good.

Dreaming big takes several steps. You have nothing to lose by believing a big dream will manifest, but you do have to follow the process. God is a God of principles—laws that control how things work. If you expect to receive more, you have to follow the right steps. The steps do not have to be in order, but mastering them is the key to success.

Step 1: *Imagine*

You must imagine yourself in the place where you want to go. Wake up like you are already doing your dream. But, in the meantime, take care of your things. If your one-bedroom apartment is not fit for a roach to live in and you are expecting to afford a six-bedroom house, back up and learn how to make your bed. You have to take care of what you have first. More comes to those who take care of the little.

Lisa Williams lived in an apartment with a deck that she decorated with patio furniture. She had a full dining-room set, including a china cabinet. Her living room was set up with a piano and sectional white furniture. She was raising two sons that knew Mama did not play. Daddy worked hard for his money, and Mama knew how to take care of him and the boys. You could eat off the floors. Not that I know anything about eating off floors, but you get the point.

On Saturday mornings, you could hear music coming from the corner window of the ground-level apartment. You could smell pine cleaner and bleach; Lisa and the boys were cleaning house. The boys could go outside later, but not until their early Saturday chores were done. Yes, that's right, boys need to clean too. Later on, you could smell good cooking. If you came over later, she would feed you.

Three years into living in that apartment, they moved into their four-bedroom home. Each of them now had their own room, and it remained spotless.

Step 2: *Prepare*

You have to be prepared to fit into where you want to go. "Bad company corrupts good manners" (2 Corinthians 15:33). What does that mean? All the home training you can get will do nothing for you if you are bent on hanging out with thugs. If your desire is to be a top executive, why are you standing on the corner with the town drug dealer? Standing there is not getting you his money nor is it preparing you to be an executive. So decide if you really want big executive money or if you just want it to remain a dream.

When you associate with someone often, you either cause him to change to be like you or you change to be like him. There is automatically some sharing going on. It is human nature to gravitate to someone that is like you. And the more you are around someone, the more the sameness is evident.

As stated in the Scripture reference above, bad company is a bad deal. All your schooling, studying, and preparation is destined for the trash if you waste time with someone who is not going where you are going, is not already where you want to go, or is trying to stay right where they are—in the gutter.

Step 3: *Action*

Donald Trump is worth about 2.9 billion dollars, according to Forbes. His income is sixty million a year. And he is ranked number seventeen on the Forbes Celebrity 100 list for 2011. Yet Trump has filed for bankruptcy protection for his business three times. Did his going bankrupt stop him? No! He always has something cooking. While in bankruptcy in his real estate business he was still on TV and still raking in the millions.

If you tap into what you have in your hands, you will always earn; you will always be up to something. What's next? Get up and do something. There is really no such thing as failure, except to those who never try. No new money is created for new millionaires. Money is transferred to those who offer what people want. There are more ideas than money. If the first try at manifesting your dream did not work, dream bigger. Before you give up, add to it. Keep going. Never quit.

Yes, you can always be broke. But as long as you are trying, that will never happen. Success comes with much activity. Learn from others who have been where you are going. You have to be bold. Sitting around talking to those who can't help you will never help you.

The point of abundance is to be who God called you to be. If your abundance is to be a millionaire, then that's your abundance. But to get there you have to keep working on something. You should always be content but never complacent. Be grateful for whatever status you have, but always embrace new opportunities when they present themselves.

Settling on making twenty thousand a year and putting forth no effort to add more income is pure and simple laziness. That's not contentment; it's trifling.

What happened to the use of your other assets? You have more than enough ideas to add more income, create a new job, and bless you and those around you.

Always be prepared to move. Opportunities present themselves daily. Be ready for yours by keeping your eyes, ears, and mind open.

Where are you right now? Are you in a place you can come back to, or are you resting on what was given to you. If you have used your faith and worked for what you have, you know how it is done. So keep moving forward. Keep moving upward. There is always a higher place.

If you are not moving, what you have now will disappear. Unless you have resigned yourself to being in retirement, there is always higher plateau.

Step 4: Give and Serve

We were all born to serve. Tell me your passion, and I will tell you how it can help others. Everything we do directly or indirectly affects another person on this planet. And we have to be good givers. How can God put a blessing in your hands when your hands are clenched around the little you have, trying to protect it. We must extend our hands and our hearts in an action of giving so that God can increase what we have.

Poverty is a mentality, and it is based on the "give me" mindset. People who are always thinking of how they can get—especially with little to no work—and never thinking of how they can give, are stuck in a poverty mindset. Their thinking is small, as it is centered only on themselves. When you expand your thinking to include others, you find that life is a circle, and it comes right back to you.

The principle of reaping and sowing is a definite. Whether you subscribe to it or not, it is truth. If you are always sowing into your future, there will always be something for you to achieve. Always. Coming back to the principle of sowing and reaping, it's not a matter of remembering it is there; it is a matter of living. If you try but do not succeed at something, that is just a part of your cycle of movement. Keep trying, or the cycle will stop. Give out and it is coming back, every time.

Ecclesiastes 11:2 admonishes you to "cast your bread upon the waters so you may find it after many days." This is different from the teaching that you should master one area and stick with it. There are so many arms to every field of study, so work on conquering all of them. If one does not work, you can fall back on the other. This is dreaming big.

Open your mind and enlarge your coast. This universe is big enough for all of God's people to prosper. Coming back from a defeat does not mean living in an alley or crashing when your unemployment runs out. Do the Donald Trump crash; do the MC Hammer crash. They both kept living large after their bumps in the road. You can always go back if you are living right. Making your coming back something to come back to!

Questions?

What are you afraid of losing?

If you succeed, what are the benefits?

If you fail this time around, what will you gain that you may not have had before? What will you lose that you could never get back?

Is chasing your dreams worth the risk? Is not chasing your dreams worth the regret?

If you fail, will you quit or try something else?

Homework

1. Do one thing this week to get you closer to your dream and four things in the next thirty days to help you get to your dream's fulfillment.

2. Do something for someone else, and ask for nothing in return.

3. Give some of your money or time to a charity.

THE POWER IN YOU

10

"If you realized how powerful your thoughts are, you would never think a negative thought."

— Peace Pilgram

The power instilled in believers after salvation is *dunamis* power. *Dunamis* is a Greek word that denotes power. It is the root of the word dynamite. In Acts 1:8, Jesus said believers will receive power after the Holy Spirit comes upon them. This is the same power He promised His followers after He arose from the dead (Mark 16:17).

Dunamis is not the same power that helps you get out of bed in the morning, take a shower, and go to work or school. It is the power that enables you to step out into unchartered territory. It is the power that takes you out of a life of sin into a person with the power to overcome previously insurmountable habits. This power is promised to all and is manifested to those who believe.

When God created Adam, he breathed in Adam's body and he became a living soul. That living being had the power to take dominion over the earth. That is exactly what God told Adam, the first man: take stewardship over the entire earth (Genesis 1:28-29). After Adam and Eve's fall from grace, they were taken out of their peaceful existence in the garden of Eden. Not until Jesus died on the cross were you given back the power to live at peace on this earth in the midst of chaos. The power was not actually imparted to you until Jesus rose from the dead and went back to His Father. Then He sent the Holy Spirit back to earth to dwell among us.

This power is here for you. It is like a brand-new Rolls Royce sitting in your garage. Unless you put some top-grade gas in it, turn on the ignition, and back it out, it will sit in the garage and rust. You are fearfully and wonderfully made, says Psalms 139: 14. Why are you sitting there until you die? The power is in you to prosper.

When Jesus began his public ministry, He had many followers. The Jewish leaders studied His ways to see if He was the King they had been promised. They looked for Jesus to reestablish the earthly kingdom they had longed for. But what Jesus told them did not satisfy their desire for an earthly kingdom that the Jews would rule. It threatened their very hierarchy. This kingdom Jesus spoke of would put all people directly under the leadership of Almighty God.

Christian teaching makes seeking the Kingdom of God seem like an unreachable goal. This is way off God's design. When you are seeking who God is, you do not have to go far. The Kingdom of God is His rule on earth through His believers. Matthew 6:33 says to seek for God's Kingdom before you get concerned about all of life's needs. After you seek Him, all the things you need concerning life will be added to you.

It is ironic that two books over in the Bible, Jesus says the kingdom of God can be found in you (Luke 17:20-21). He says that you cannot seek it with your natural eyes, because it is in you. You have to perceive it with your spiritual eyes. You want power? It is in you. You are already great.

There are secrets to operating in this invisible kingdom, and this way of living is talked about in 1 Corinthians 2:1-16. It is a spiritual kingdom with massive power, given to you when you acknowledge Christ as your savior. People who think the kingdom is only material things are mistaken. God takes care of unbelievers just as He does believers. But believers are given the keys to access the mysteries in the kingdom. They are revealed through the Word of God and your relationship to Him.

There is a branch of study in physics called dynamics. This field of study focuses on the actions of forces on bodies either in motion or at rest. Dynamics relate to you in this way: the dunamis given to you is the activator that causes regular situations to be turned into the miraculous. This is the stuff talked about in Ephesians 3:20 that says that God will do far beyond what (you) ask or can even think, based on the power (dunamis) at work in you. To live in this realm, you have to be a believer, and you have to walk in your faith. Nobody has more faith than you; you and everyone else was given a measure of faith. All were given the same measure of faith. You have the measure needed to transform your average life into a magnificent one.

You may be one of those people that handles money like it is a cure-all. When the money does not rush in the direction you are going, you get discouraged. This way is fruitless, because it is in opposition to God's principle regarding power. You are called to invest what has been given to you and to expect God to explode it with the dunamis in you. You do not need money to get started; all you need is the power you already have.

There is a law in physics that says a body in motion stays in motion. If you tap into the source that will keep you moving forward, you will never worry again about being stagnant, discontented, or running your well dry. Inside you is a well of living water that springs forth all the way to everlasting life. If you have already drunk of the water offered to you in Christ, you will never to be thirsty again (John 4:14). That's His promise. You have rivers of living water inside you; all you have to do is believe and tap in. Continuously tapping in keeps the waters running.

When you make the decision to bring your imagination to light God will do more than you ever expected. It is those bold people that turn a little idea into a fortune 500 company. You have to make a demand on the little dream and it will grow. Never cast off that dream as not worth anything. By speaking or writing or meditating on your dream you are making the decision to bring your dream out of the darkness

If you do not live in expectation, you will not see when you have increased. Every step in the direction of your dream should be filled with anticipation.

You can do all the right actions without knowledge of the power God has put in you. But without recognizing the power working at work, you will get few results and a multitude of frustration. The power in you is your portion of God. It is waiting for your faith connection. Your faith joining forces with the almighty God automatically puts you in the arena of the successful. The only separation between you and your faith is your independence. Acknowledge that you need what is inside, and it will appear. God is waiting to hear your request for assistance.

Without this connection, you will be working hard all your life with results that make you work even harder. This is not God's plan for your life. God's plan is for you to prosper. God's desire is for you to flourish and have favorable results in all you put your hands to. He specializes in the great. If you have already trusted God to change your life, then He wants you to translate that into your everyday walk.

What did you think God had in mind for you from the time you were born until the time you die? All these beautiful creations were not set up just for you to enjoy from a distance. Prosperity is yours for the taking. You can have it only by lighting the dynamite that resides in you. You are much stronger than you think.

If you are waiting to feel the power of your success, it is not going to happen. Faith without works is dead (James 2; 17). You only sense the power when you start believing and start acting. Do not wait, ask for manifested power today.

Oasis Family Life Church is a spiritual body of believers. It is an oasis for many families living in Paulding County, Georgia area. But the building that houses this body of believers is an expression of the transformation that is taking place in the lives of the members. It is a statement of the inward blessing.

I could conduct services in an open field, but the Oasis Family Life Church structure was made for the comfort of parishioners and a welcoming atmosphere for visitors. It's the same with your personal life. God gives you the power to get wealth (Deuteronomy 8:18). Accepting Christ and then spending the rest of your days sitting in a sanctuary is unrealistic. You are designed to take over this earth; prosperity is for all. And God wants prosperity you can see. The children of Israel were prosperous even as they walked around in the wilderness. First they left Egypt with all of the precious metals they could gather. During the forty years they wandered in the wilderness, God provided their food and drink, and their shoes never wore out. How much did they pay to eat or drink? How much did their shoes cost?

God can prosper you with or without money. But a lowly existence is not the picture God wants for his people. God wants you to soar like an eagle and run like a deer. Why is prosperity for some and not for you? After all, there is nothing you can do that would cause God to stop loving you.

Wealth is not money. Wealth is the accumulation of assets. So running after money is not at all what I am talking about. Be honest with yourself: living in constant want of basic necessities is no way to live. Continually searching for a handout is the plight of the mediocre. That's not your best life. Choose today to tap into the power in you.

Winning the lottery will not give you prosperity. It was already given to you when you joined the family of believers. Besides, a million-dollar payout does not make you a millionaire. After you pay the taxes on a million dollars it is not a million any more. Your power is in you. The power you are tapping into is God Himself. This is not a pipe dream. This is your life. Your weakness is God's strength (2 Corinthians 12:9). Have you asked for the revealed power of God to manifest in your life today?

This is the same power that propels an abused child to move up the ranks to national stardom; an orphan child to die a millionaire, leaving a legacy of great philanthropy; and a deaf and mute child to learn to read at four, graduate with honors from college, and give inspirational addresses in several countries.

All of this power is in the kingdom of God. If you seek the kingdom daily, you will find it. Because you are reading this, it is for you. You are meant to experience the life that was designed just for you. You have family members waiting for your leadership. Be the change that you are looking for.

What is in your hand? What are you working with? It is all in you and has been since the beginning. You are blessed to be a blessing. Use the power in you!

God said to Abraham, "I will make you a great nation, and I will bless you and make your name great; and you shall be a blessing" (Genesis 12:2). And Paul wrote, "You are all one in Christ. And if you belong to Christ then you are Abraham's seed, and heirs according to the promise" (Galatians 3:29).

Questions?

Are you using the power given to you by God? In what ways?

What power do you have that you haven't tapped into? How will you tap into it?

Name three ways that you can use your power to help you accomplish your dreams.

GOD, FAMILY & FOOTBALL

11

"Wise are those who learn that the bottom line doesn't always have to be their top priority."
— William Arthur Ward

The Bible says, "But seek ye first the kingdom of God, and his righteousness; and all these things shall be added unto you" (Matthew 6:33). God is all about priorities and leading a balanced life. As long as you are in the will of God—following His plan for your life—and you have the right motives, you are seeking His kingdom first. Your life will be an example for others of God's grace and goodness.

Vince Lombardi, the popular coach of the Green Bay Packers, was the face of football in the early sixties. He is one of the most quoted people of all time. He guided his players with one theme: "There are only three things that are important in your life: your God, your family, and the Green Bay Packers." He understood the importance of prioritizing and finding balance when chasing after dreams. He was such a great inspiration that the Super Bowl trophy is called the Lombardi Trophy.

Lombardi's ideas about success were many, but his main one was the importance of focus. His winning record and the loyalty of his players to his ideals would not have been evident without his focus. With a wife and two children as a backdrop, he lived and dreamed in pigskin. Nearing the end of his life, he wondered if he had been a good father. His daughter questioned the ups and downs of his personality, but she later came to realize she lived a life of privilege and her father really loved her. His only son also came to terms with their relationship and became a well-traveled speaker on leadership and is currently an NFL analyst. When you are driven, it is easy to lose focus on what is important, but it's never too late to get it together.

Lombardi's early training was in the Catholic Church, and he wanted to be a priest. But in his young adulthood, he realized he could be more effective as a coach than as a priest. He was a driven man who excelled greatly as a coach in the National Football League.

Focus is not one-dimensional, as the world implies. You are made in the likeness and image of God. And God is a lot more than one-dimensional. He created the entire universe all by Himself. You have to live your life in the multifaceted world and focus on God, family, and your dream, but at times each will place different demands on you. You have to know where to place your energy while balancing the others and not letting them slip. A person who always emphasizes one area is out of focus.

God made us with the ability to put things into perspective. If He is not first, everything else flounders. You are not successful if you have many assets but are suffering with ulcers because of stress. Where is the balance in that? If God is not first, He will not be last. Your aim for success has been voided from the start.

Let's discuss the balance God not only expects from you but is requiring of you if you are to live at peace with the universe. When you are at peace with the universe, you have peace with God, others, and yourself. So read on, and affirm that the following ways are already your ways, or adjust your life to line up with the most important things in life.

God

This is not a book on religion, but to understand the reason for everything, you have to begin with God. He created it all. If you want to know how to get from where you are now to where you are trying to go, you must know it all starts and ends with God. God made you.

In the beginning, God created everything. Then He created you (Adam actually). He told Adam to run everything; He gave Adam responsibility for everything on this earth. God gave him dominion. After Adam and Eve's disobedience, the perfect world was shaken. Humans then had to struggle to survive. Hard work was introduced.

All the while, God was devising a plan to rescue you from yourself. His dream for you came true in the person of Jesus Christ. His only son would put you back in perfect standing with Him. All you have to do is believe and accept what Jesus did, and you receive back the prosperity that was yours from the beginning.

So Jesus was sent just to show you how to live, and then He died on the cross. Then He sent His Spirit to empower you to have the abundance you were entitled to. You simply have to believe He did this for you. And that is it, pure and simple.

The only roadblock is the one that occurs in your mind. That's one you receive from the enemy. Believing in the truth is the only way back to your wealthy place.

God loves you so much that He rescues you, even when you mess yourself up. Every day you must refresh your mind to what God has already done for you. The right way to think is to believe God really did this for you and that you got it. It is okay to have a lapse of memory sometimes; just remember to come back. Renew your mind every day. Remember the present! Be present in the present, and do not worry about tomorrow or your ugly past. Prepare for your most excellent future.

Never forget to thank God regularly for what He did. He loves that. When you begin to thank God, you can actually feel His presence. His power embraces you, and you can conquer more than you set out to do. Being grateful helps you stay grounded and humble. It reminds you that you are a servant and that everything is a gift.

Well, that's the end of the first step in your gaining balance. Keep God first, and all your plans will be successful. If you want to understand this way for yourself, read the Holy Bible. All of this is in there. If you read it enough, these principles will stick and become a way of life. It will save you from some unnecessary mistakes. No, you are not perfect, but if you decide to work for this perfect God, He will direct all your steps when you acknowledge that He can.

God expects you to live in abundance with the help His son gives. Anything less than that should be unacceptable to you. Pay that other voice no attention. That's just the other presence on this earth that only wants to steal, kill, and destroy God's plans. But guess what, he is a created being too. Unlike horror movies, in the real world created beings have no power over their creator, God.

Family

God loves family. After He created Adam from the dust of the earth and gave him dominion over all of the earth, he said there was no way man should enjoy all that alone. He created a woman, starting with Adam's rib. He said the woman would help the man in the domination of the earth.

She was called Eve because she is the mother of all living. If you want something to have life and look good, add a woman's touch. Let a man who is struggling in his spirit get touched (sorry, wrong book!). Anyway, it was definitely not good for man to be alone. The woman was made for man. He could not handle being alone.

God loves company, so he created man and woman to be like Him. He could watch them from heaven and enjoy them enjoying each other's company and the earth He created for their pleasure. All of this gives Him glory.

Each person cohabiting peacefully with others is part of the family God originally intended for this earth. The second piece of the puzzle to creating bigger dreams is living in harmony with others. Your family should be more important than any big dream you could ever capture. Take the family out of perspective, and a person is out of balance.

DREAMSPIRATION

Chantell was a dreamer. She made some questionable decisions as a teenager, but once she defined herself and her dreams, she decided to go big. Going back to school would be difficult because she was a single mother, but she knew that it was the only way she could accomplish her dream of being a nurse. The opportunity came for her to go to school, and she prayed about it and trusted God.

Chantell started school, and it was hard for her to balance work, school, and motherhood. She was also an involved member at her church. The women there saw how focused and determined she was to accomplish her dream, so they pitched in during the week, watching her son when she had evening classes or had to work late. When she got home, no matter how tired or how late, she made a point to go over her son's homework, sign his daily class schedule and write and respond to notes from his teachers. She cleared her schedule whenever possible to attend parent-teacher conferences, and she supported him in his extra-curricular activities.

When a friend asked Chantell, "When do you have time for yourself?" she said, "Every day!" Every day when she went to class or did her homework, projects, or labs, she was doing something for herself. That's why it was so important for her to go the extra mile for her son; she was already going the extra mile for herself. It was a sacrifice she made so her dream could be realized. Accomplishing her dreams was a personal thing for her.

Chantell graduated with a degree in nursing and became an RN. She loved what she did with a passion, and once her dream came true, she couldn't see herself being anything better, because she was living her purpose.

Stay in balance with your plan, and you will have real prosperity. Wealth not shared with family is not conducive with living peaceably in this world: treat others like you want to be treated. This treatment, or love, is to begin at home.

I guess I will stop here and explain family. A traditional family is a husband and wife and children. But God knew that the human definition of family would change. That is why He extended the definition more than two thousand years ago.

If you read in Mark starting at chapter ten, verse ten, you will see that God promised something to every person that chooses Him as their guide: an extended family that is not made up of blood relatives. A single person can answer the call to family by treating others as he or she would want to be treated—by sharing with neighbors, friends, and the less fortunate.

All humans are included in family and especially those that are believers in this way of living. So taking care of family is a priority for any person who dreams big and expects to stay in unity with the laws governing the universe. Sharing your life with family is the way you were created to exist in this universe. Any other design is going against the laws of nature and causes a lack of peace.

Simply put, God is our father, and we are all sisters and brothers. You want to know who to share with? Start with those you live with, and then spread out to those in close proximity. If you are really tapped in, create causes that can bless those you do not even know. When you can do that, you know you have crossed past the line of mediocrity.

Football

I played in high school, and I was pretty good at it. (And recently that pounding decided to make its presence known in my body. Football is a rough sport.) I had letters from colleges trying to recruit me, so I believe I could have assisted some college team somewhere. But that was not my dream or the dream God had for me.

Do not let anyone talk you into doing something that is not designed for you. If you never thought of something, yet someone whispers that it is what you are supposed to be doing, put it on a shelf. I won't say to throw it away; hold it just in case. If you don't ever feel compelled to pursue it and you never hear about it again, then it was never for you.

God first, family next, and big dreaming last is your direction. If you follow these steps, following your dream will never be a problem. You may make some missteps, but not many.

All three of these at the same time can be overwhelming, but don't get frustrated. I was a youth pastor when I got married and began a family. All my passions were growing at the same time. My wife is flourishing in her personal ministries; my children are thriving in school and life; and God is prospering Oasis Family Life Church. This is all happening simultaneously. I am focusing on all three at the same time. I am in balance. Thank God.

You have to understand something. Once you set the foundation for anything to grow luxuriously, the hardest work is done. After the foundation is laid, it is guaranteed to stand with some patient attention. When a dream is put into perspective, it is placed in the arena where it is supposed to be. Selfish aspirations make for an eventual unhappy you. Keep everything in proper balance, and the universe will see to it that it remains and thrives.

It's like the tree that is planted by the rivers of water. It brings its fruit in the right season, when it is the most beneficial; its leaves never whither. The winds come, and it still stands strong.

You can't dream bigger if you have not mastered the small. Oasis Family Life Church started in a high school cafeteria. Children's Church was in one of the classrooms. The greeters stood on the ramp leading to the side door to the cafeteria. The church "auditorium" had to be set up and broken down every time we gathered. We enjoyed each other like we were in a big cathedral. At that time, having an office was not a priority. My office was my cell phone in my car or in my living room.

Surroundings cannot stop big dreaming. Successful dreamers are believers. With God at the helm, you can't help but prosper. Add the love for family, and then start working. And remember that faith is your first asset. "Now faith is the substance of things hoped for and the evidence of things not seen" (Hebrews 11:1).

Substance—physical matter—is in your imagination and so is the proof that what you are hoping for is real. This is where big dreaming begins and ends. Let your faith work for you.

All successful people have the same theme: God, family, and their big dreams manifested.

Questions?

Is your life balanced? If not, what is out of balance?

What comes first in your life, and where do you focus your time? God, Family, Work, Education, Relationship, Other _____

How can you achieve the proper balance of putting God, family, and dreams on top?

What pressures force you to place something before your family or God?

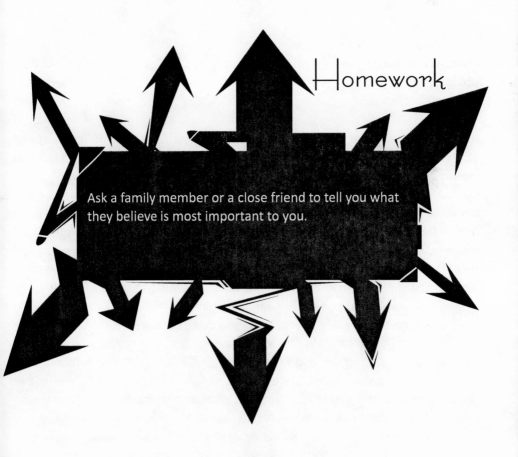

Homework

Ask a family member or a close friend to tell you what they believe is most important to you.

THINK MULTIPLICATION

12

"Giving people a little more than they expect is a good way to get back more than you'd expect."

— *Robert Half*

G od is a God of multiplication. When you think God, think more. Whatever God has given you, He expects you to share with others, so that it can multiply. What you start in faith, God will finish with abundance.

One church cliché is "If God never does another thing for me, He has already done enough." In principle, that is true, because the work was complete before the world was framed. But you should always be expanding. You should never be complacent. If you still have the strength to do something, you should be doing something. At eighty years old, after coming out of the wilderness and headed toward the Promised Land, Joshua proclaimed that he had the same strength he always had and still wanted his mountain.

In Luke 19 is a story of a landowner leaving his ten servants to go to a far country. He left them each with talents to use in his absence. When he returned, he called a meeting to check on the progress of his talents. The servants with ten and five talents had invested the talents wisely and doubled their worth. But the servant with one talent had buried it for fear that he might do the wrong thing with it. He was not rewarded for his stewardship; he was rebuked as a lazy servant. His one talent was taken and given to the one who had started out with ten.

Now, in a finite mind, that does make sense. But you can read it for yourself. The point of the story is that everyone has been given something to work with. There is no excuse for anyone to sit around waiting for a handout, and if something is given to you, no matter how small it may seem, you have the power to multiply it.

God is always adding. When the number gets too big, the equation turns to multiplication. For every act of obedience, there is a guarantee of multiplication far beyond the investment. When you read about the tithe and offerings in Malachi 3, you see the promise that your offering will turn into a blessing too big to contain. When Abraham was told to leave his country and kinsman, he was promised that his seed would multiply to more than the stars. He would be blessed, and he would be a blessing (Genesis 12). Jesus said that when you give it will be given back to you in good measure, pressed down, and shaken together (Luke 6:38). Everywhere you look in God's word, multiplication is taking place.

God will always exceed your expectations. You have to think multiplication. You do not have to look for Him to create something new for you. It is already in existence; you just have not seen it. You know you want more. You are content and grateful for all that has been given, but you cannot settle when you are still here.

There is no investment firm in this entire world that gives you a forty, sixty, or one hundred percent return. The only way to reap those returns is in your giving. The problem believers have had with giving is their reluctance to look for a return. Return of investment is what God does. God is more interested in your heart toward Him than in any amount you give away. That is why He is so willing to multiply everything you give. He simply wants a relationship with you. Your relationship with Him is your investment. That's why He guarantees such a phenomenal return.

You are rewarded for your dreaming. If you are not dreaming big, you will not give big. If you are not giving big, you will not receive big. If you are not receiving big, you are in a cycle that you need to break.

In Mark 10, it is said that all who leave family and possessions to follow Christ will receive all of it back, including houses and land—plus eternal life. You will be persecuted for this sacrifice, but it is well worth the risk. There is an answer for any hardship that you may face. For every temptation not to believe, God has made a way for you to escape. The escape is your physical act of faith. It is a principle that cannot fail.

I am not sure what happened a few generations ago with the principle of expectation, but its absence did nothing to the dreamers. The dreamers kept putting out and receiving. Those that quit dreaming lived in necessity.

God is constantly calling for increase. He promises increase. He is the one that gives increase. You cannot increase yourself. Well, you can, but you will be fighting to keep it all the days of your life. But God's increase is permanent. Once you taste it, you will never go back.

When your faith has been activated and you actually experience God's increase, it is nearly impossible to live an average life again. While you are here, you should never have the "I have arrived" mindset. You will arrive when you are called from this life into eternity. But while you are here, you are expected to continue to multiply.

You are supposed to use up every resource that you have. Multiplication does not happen when you hold back. "If you save your life, you will lose it and if you lose your life, you will save it" (Luke 17:33). You have to extend yourself to expand yourself.

Oasis Family Life Church has grown hundreds of times over from its beginnings, but I will not be satisfied until God tells me to stop. God will not tell me to stop my actions toward expanding His kingdom. His kingdom is supposed to cover the earth. My ministry will expand as long as my faith is expanding. When God stops moving, I will stop moving.

Believers are the salt of the earth. Until the entire earth has been seasoned, there is more work to be done. Your dream is not big enough if it expands only to your front door.

You are blessed to be a blessing. When you really are blessed, you can't help but want to see others blessed. That's the expansion of a dream. Multiply what you are thinking; when your dream starts to manifest, add to it. You do not have to reinvent the wheel. And this is not fairytale stuff. This is real. God's Word has not changed and neither has His desire for you. Multiplication is in your DNA.

My last thought on this topic is the problem with family members. Some believers do not believe in the prosperity message. The Scriptures are not for private interpretation. I speak from experience. I have seen what God can do. He has done it for me and for countless others who dared to believe. Do not be left behind because of the voices of those that are afraid to change. You change, and prove them wrong.

There is no such thing as the prosperity gospel. This is the gospel of grace. Grace is God's undeserved favor. This is the reward for everyone that enters through the gate of Jesus Christ. It is God's desire for you to have the kingdom. It gives Him pleasure to see you walk in His promises (Luke 12:32). Perceive what is in you, and give to multiply. If you put nothing out, nothing will come back.

The old Billy Preston song "Nothing From Nothing Leaves Nothing" is proper math. But it does not apply to what you have inside. God did not leave you empty handed. Your gifts and talents—no matter how small they are to you—become much when put out to the light of day and expanded in the Master's hand.

A few years ago, a small church was getting ready to purchase a new structure. Many of the members pledged a thousand-dollar seed to assist with the move. One member knew that she did not have the money, and she did not know how she would get it. She decided to purpose in her heart to get it and to trust God for the increase.

Her promise was to give the pledge in thirty days. In less than two weeks, her job decided to change the way they paid the non-officer positions. Because of this change, every employee in her department was taken from hourly to salary. This resulted in an immediate refund of held payroll in the form of two weeks' worth of pay. Her refund check was 1,500 dollars. Her step of faith blessed hundreds of families.

Cathy Taylor worked at a bank in Atlanta that gave profit-sharing checks to all employees in January, based on the bank's performance the previous year. When the economy began to falter, the top executives decided in August that there would be no profit sharing that coming January. Cathy refused to believe that and asked all those that would pray to believe with her for a reversal in the decision. No word was given about the matter. When the end of January came, profit-sharing checks were handed out to all the employees.

Nancy Phelps bought a business that was dying. As a believer, she walked in faith every day. She continued giving off the income she received and trusted God for the success of the business. In two years, the business was featured in a large-circulation magazine, and the company was hired to do business in a million dollar industry.

Your expansion is based on your performance in faith and giving. And your miraculous expansion will always include blessing those around you.

Never think small when you dream and give. If you want your dream to expand, make sure your dreams include expanding God's kingdom. It is God's job to expand. You can plant the dream and you can water it, but God is the one who gives the increase.

Questions?

At what level is your faith when it comes to the principles of giving?

What, if anything, scares you the most about giving?

How important is it for you to advance God's kingdom?

Do you feel that you are doing your part in regard to giving? If not, what can you do?

Do you tithe, give, and save? If you do, how much and how often?

Do you plan your finances and follow good stewardship principles?

THE SOUND OF PROSPERITY

13

"Prosperity is a way of living and thinking, and not just money or things."
— Eric Butterworth

A friend of mine heard me talk about prosperity and became excited. The day he decided to look for it, an older woman gave him an awakening that directed him in the opposite way. Unfortunately, he heard what prosperity is *not* before experiencing what it is.

He and this neighbor were having a conversation about a charity organization. Then the woman began to complain about how often they asked for money from the public. They had recently asked for a twenty five dollar donation and even though she had received assistance from them in the past, she complained that the amount of donations they received from the government and the public should be more than enough to last a year. "They need to understand that times are hard, and everybody ain't got no money! They are going to use that money to stuff their pockets. That ain't nothing but a scam to get some more money!" My friend attempted to correct and encourage her, but she obviously had spoken this language for some time. His efforts were meaningless. He ended the conversation and returned to work.

My friend went back to his desk and wrote a note: "This was obviously not the sound of prosperity!" Well, I agree. It was poverty in its perfect form. Prosperity is in total dependence on God. The aura of prosperity brings God's increase to all that you do. You do not complain about nickels and dimes and what you do not have. You thank God for what you do have, you give, and you expect increase in your life.

Prosperity is a way of thinking and living. People in poverty do something that is obvious to those around them: they depend on people and systems to take care of them.

Tony Jackson became really perturbed when he found out his sister had hit the lottery. His problem was that she did not offer him a portion. She knew that he had eight children and a wife and that he lived in the poorest part of town. There she was, gainfully employed with two children and living in a private residence.

Tony's sister did not owe him a red cent. What did her winnings have to do with his issues? She could have been nice if she wanted to. But did he know her situation? He was just worried about his and where the next handout would come from. That was not his sister's problem.

Now, you could say that she could have at least given him a couple of hundred. Yes, she could have. But she was not obligated to take care of him. The fact that this was his train of thought bothers me; instead he should have been happy for her. But he had come to expect her charitable giving. He should not have a sense of entitlement about her money, but instead the desire to obtain his own.

The sound of prosperity rings from a heart filled with faith and from believing that principles work. You live in an arena of expectation from God and not individuals. You know when you give that it is coming back to you multiplied. People will give to you, but you do not know who. You do not covet what your neighbor has, what your sister has, or what your cousin has. You live in your own big dreams. You want what is yours to multiply so that you can be numbered with the ones who give regularly to others.

Proverbs 22:3 tells you that a wise man sees what is coming ahead and plans, but a simple man just prods along in life and is punished for it. This is the reason you should save: there will always be lean times as well as prosperous times. That translates to seed time and harvest time. That's the sound of prosperity, a person who knows how to steward what God has provided. You will be able to give when others falter.

In prosperity you do not complain about your job; you thank God that you have one. Complainers stay in poverty. You have dominion over this earth, so what are you complaining about? You have in your hand the power to get wealth. Your sound makes the noise of increase. You don't say things like "That girl took my job!" You thank God for the opportunity to get a better job, or you examine yourself and take responsibility for your mistakes.

When you know how to stay right on beat like a good drummer, you are surrounded by the harmony of prosperity. Your arrival is marked by your air, and your accomplishments are in the atmosphere around you. You are not boasting, and you are not arrogant. You are walking in the confidence that you know who you are in God's kingdom. Your sound says that you are where you are supposed to be. You are walking and blending in the right place. It is here where your provisions meet your vision. You have walked into your dream, and God manifests all the needs to sustain it.

Ignorance of the Word has caused many people to think of prosperity as a materialistic way of living. This is far from the truth. Prosperity is actually the opposite of materialism. Poverty is more materialistic than prosperity .

A person with a materialistic mindset always wants things to prove his or her worth. A poverty mindset will make you gravitate to filling your life with stuff to fake prosperity. Prosperity-minded people gravitate to God and allow Him to direct their lives. Your life in prosperity is filled with the manifested desires of your heart (Psalms 37:4).

REFLECTIONS

ARE YOU A GIVER OR TAKER?

1. Do you look for ways to get things free, even if you could be breaking the law?

2. Would you lie if it meant that you could get something out of it?

3. Are you happier when you receive something than when you give?

4. Have you ever volunteered or helped a charity or nonprofit?

5. When was the last time you donated money or something new to a charity?

6. When was the last time you received from a charity?

7. Do you depend on gifts for your survival, though you are not disabled or sick?

If you answered yes to 1, 2, 3 or 7, or if your answer to 5 was "never" or "a long time ago", then you need to come out of the poverty mindset. Find a way to do something for someone else. Give more of your money, time, and possessions. Not only will it feel good, it will bring increase to you. After all, "It is more blessed to give than to receive" (Acts 20:35).

It is never too late to change, though as you age, change is harder. You will probably have to change your friends; you may even have to lessen some family ties. If you stop hanging out with that poverty-minded brother, he will still be your brother. That will not change. In Mark 10, I hear that Jesus promises to give a hundredfold return of mothers and sisters and brothers and houses and lands to all those that leave theirs for the sake of the gospel (that's the same gospel that holds a guarantee of health and wealth). This is in addition to eternal life.

The day you understand is the day you should walk into it. If you aim to please those around you, you will always stay the same. Your place in prosperity is waiting for you to hit the right note.

I had the privilege of being around some prosperous people during my early years of dreaming. I knew that I was reaching for the stars where they lived, and I knew that what they were saying was what I needed to hear. I began to join their noise. I disconnected from those that irritated my spirit. Actually, my sound was irritating to them, so many left me. Thank God—less emotional stress for me.

Unfortunately, it is very hard for people who have lived in poverty for thirty and forty years to change. It is not impossible, but old habits die hard. Renewing your mind is not easy.

If you Google the word prosperous, you will find several definitions. But the best fit with this topic is "auspicious." Auspicious means that you have what it takes to be successful now and in the future. Auspicious people are the philanthropists. They are the proprietors. They support the needy and human services. They walk in favor. The wealthiest have wings of hospitals named after them. Their names emit respect, and their sound never diminishes.

You can hear prosperity walking down Park Avenue in midtown Manhattan. There is an air, a breeze, a sense of peace and well-being. If you are tapped in and seeking it, you will recognize its essence. You can detect the aroma, the atmosphere, the moment you step into it.

If you live in the frequency of prosperity, any other frequency is a distraction. You can discern the change in channels, and the static disturbs your peace of mind. When you become aware of the purpose of prosperity and have been a recipient of that grace, you never go back.

Poverty is an enemy of prosperity. The two cannot live together. Since God brought me into this light, I have never desired to live another way. I have always aspired for the ministry God gave me to continuously increase. I am not satisfied with the least. When Oasis Family Life was established, God breathed prosperity on it, and prosperity has followed from the beginning.

Poverty and prosperity will never walk together. They do not agree.

Prosperity is total dependence on God, and poverty is not. Poverty lacks the faith needed to prosper. How can you go after your big dreams if you do not believe? Faith is the substance of things you hope for; you cannot make a request to God if you do not believe that He exists and will reward you for seeking Him (Hebrews 11:1-3).

Going after your dreams is going after the God in you. You are fearfully and wonderfully made. To reside in any other frequency than your prosperity is a fight against the call on your life. But this direction can be followed only in faith. If you believe in God, believe that He has a prosperous life designed for you and that it is time to fight for it.

Make sure the sound of prosperity rings in your ear every day. Your faith is developed by what you hear. Make sure you tune in to the right station. Stay away from the other sounds. Get away from those yapping it up about struggling. "Bad company corrupts good manners" (I Cor. 15:33). Do not waste your time with those that do not want to go. Create your own prosperous sound; those listening for that sound will find you.

When you are finally resting in your prosperous place, do not forget how you got there: "It is God who gives you power to get wealth" (Deuteronomy 8:18). Live in thanksgiving, and continue to give. God cannot resist the sound of your praise. That's the undeniable sound of your prosperity.

Questions?

Are you living a prosperous life or a materialistic one? Explain your answer.

Are you around people who have a prosperous mind or poverty mind? How does either effect you?

Do you complain about your situation instead of actively doing something to change it? Explain your answer.

Are you ready to live in prosperity, or do you feel like it's not that easy? Explain your answer

PART

3

Moving
Forward

YOU'VE GOT NOW

14

"Procrastination is the thief of time."

— *Edward Young*

You must understand that when God gives you a dream, it is for now. As soon as you dream, you have to take on the characteristic of what you dreamed.

If a young girl at twelve dreams of being Miss America, she can't start playing hooky at thirteen and smoking at fourteen, and decide to drop out of school at sixteen. Where do you think that dream of Miss America will end up? It will be given to the girl who dares to prepare while envisioning her dream.

The prize for Miss America is already prepared: world travel as a spokesperson for her cause along with scholarship money. So where does getting high and all-night partying come in?

In eternity, where God lives, the beginning and the end are one. When you begin to dream, you have already won. Your life has to catch up to your dream, and that takes faith and obedience. Discipline is the ammunition for successful endings. Obey the plans. You do not have to reinvent the wheel; just follow the plan that is already set.

If you are at the gym in line for the next pickup basketball game, you cannot leave to go take a nap. Your next is now. When it is time to step onto the court, nobody is going to wait for you. It will be now for the person who has prepared and is ready to play.

When I think of the British royalty, this concept comes to life. Prince Charles does not run around wreaking havoc in his family. He lives like a royal, associates with royals, and receives all the benefits of being royalty.

Royals who do not play the part get banned from the royal circle. Yes, they may get a separation stipend for being part of the royal family, but there is no chance of being next. Royals who do not yet sit on the throne still carry the weight of the monarchy because of who they are. Royalty is what royalty does. They practice royalty every day. When they do not the world knows about it. Royalty carries a lot of weight.

I cannot see Prince William break dancing in the middle of Times Square on a cardboard box. He is second in line to the British throne. He's not going to knowingly do that and jeopardize his reputation. All he has is now, not next. Reputations are built every day not just one.

Although Princess Diana was divorced from Prince Charles, she lived lavishly and floated easily within the upper echelon of society. When she died, her funeral was parallel to those reserved for heads of state. Her royal status did not dim. Her opportunity for now was every day of her life.

See yourself the same way, because that is how God sees you. He is waiting on your response to the dream He gave you. Now I must mention the poverty mindset again. You may be waiting on somebody else to give you something that will propel you out of obscurity. That's the poverty mindset. It says you must wait for a handout. Where is the faith in that? Your prosperity is already guaranteed. You inherited it when you made the decision to join God's kingdom.

Living in your dream now keeps you alert and excited. You do not have to be jealous of anyone else, because there is room for every dream that God inspires.

Your understanding of the next-is-now principle gets instant results when you believe. You begin to look at yourself differently. You begin to act and talk differently. Your turn is now. No more next. The word next encourages procrastination. For this season, when time is speeding up, next gives you the impression that you are waiting for something. What are you waiting for?

Give yourself a paradigm shift. You are not waiting on anything. Your dream has already been completed in eternity. It is waiting for you to understand that it is for now.

As soon as the dream comes into focus, you have to begin to walk toward it. There's no getting ready to start. Just start. When you wait to adjust your mind, you give yourself time to revert to old habits. A paradigm shift is one of those miracles that happens as soon as you latch onto live in faith. You start to change, because now you believe that the dream is real. It's when you do not believe that you drag your feet and continue as if nothing ever happened.

Dreaming the now dream should be a part of every decision you make: taking on a new job, getting married, starting a family, changing careers, and so on. "Now faith is the substance of things hoped for the evidence of things not seen" (Hebrews 11:1).

Don't take your future for granted. Always acknowledge God in your decision-making process. He has prepared a prosperous life for you inside your dream. He is the author and finisher of your faith.

The action that makes the measure of faith given to you come alive will never manifest without dreaming. There are so many great and wonderful things that God has laid up for you. They are not for later but for now.

A young couple got married without the benefit of premarital counseling. The wife had two children from a previous relationship. Their mistake of not planning how they would conduct the family turned ugly soon after the initial wedded bliss. The nightmare of unplanned steps shook their young marriage.

The wife usually spent the holidays and summer vacation with her immediate family, and neither of them thought that the husband and children were now a new "immediate family." The first summer holiday rolled around, and she prepared for the family to go on vacation. They had their first big blowout when her husband discovered that his wishes were not considered when the plans were made. He felt slighted and could not adjust his attitude enough to accompany his new family.

Overlooking small things is what can spoil a beautiful picture. Their very first holiday outing as a family was tarnished by an assumption.

When a dream comes into view, it's time for planning. Now! If the young couple had sat down and not fantasized about being together but planned their future together, the first holiday would have been a blast.

I will not turn this into a chapter about premarital advice, but you must know that God is concerned about everything that concerns you. When is the right time to create new traditions for a new family? Now! As soon as it is obvious that a marriage is in the future, planning should begin. Gazing at the fairytale marriage of television personalities does nothing for your marriage. You did not have premarital counseling? So what? Start over today. Dream together. And dream big.

The point of this story is that now is the time for plans. You can't wait until you are manifesting your dream into reality. When the wedding plans are being made, it's time to sit and dream about the future. Get past the cliché of two kids and a dog. What about childhood activities, private school, and college? These lifestyles do not just happen. Take the steps in preparation for the miraculous.

There is a strong possibility that waiting on next may put your dream so far off into the future that it never happens. It's a sad ending when a person dies never realizing any part of his or her dream. You may not have the luxury of a trust fund from Daddy or a very supportive family. Your surroundings may not be conducive to encouraging your dreams. What better time to dream than when things seem hopeless? How did Tyler Perry go from abuse and homelessness to being one of the premiere players in Hollywood?

Train your children to dream and act now. They can't wait to get to college to get their first A. It is always now. Every moment counts. Every step is important. Interaction with teachers can prove invaluable when they need a referral for college or employment. If you do not tell them about now, they may think that what they do today is not important because they have a long time to fix things.

There is no worse situation than coming to an appointed time and not being prepared. When I started Club VFL at my father's church, God gave me an innovative plan from day one. The first few young people that came thought that they were coming to a real club. I had strobe lights on, and the house lights were turned off. The music blared. And the singing was off the chain; God had sent some singers that were either professional or would be soon. God always knows!

I did not wait until we were ministering to over three hundred youths every week to institute Jerry Springer-like formats with such subject matter as "How can I have a peaceful relationship with my stepfather?" The young people were encouraged to come just as they were. We had to hire law enforcement personnel for security because of the charged atmosphere among youth bused in from both sides of the tracks.

Over five years that Club VFL existed it ministered to some three thousand young people. But the concept was birthed immediately when I was given the charge to start a youth ministry. I did not wait until all was perfectly in line. I started with what I had. The time was right at that moment. There was no six months of planning. I started with what I had—a dream and a location.

They came in their street gear and attitudes. Clashes of neighborhoods threatened to start a riot, but God had me change it into friendly competition. "Who can bring the most people to the club?"

This setting revolutionized the lives of many who were looking for a change. The unction to make "now" changes is what pushed Club VFL to the top as the most cutting edge youth gathering in the Atlanta area.

Now is immediate. If you wait until tomorrow, your now may never come.

Decide today what needs some now attention, and get started. God needs only a small step to open up a big door. What door are you leaving shut because you fail to act now?

"I got next!" was a saying for the previous century. God said many things, but what is He saying now? Remind yourself of what He did previously, but update it with what He is doing for you now. The work is already complete. The now is for you. Make it happen now!

"Today if you will hear his voice, harden not your hearts."
– Hebrews 3:7-8

Questions?

Are you operating in the *now*? If not, what is stopping you?

What is the biggest missing piece that keeps you from accomplishing your dreams?

Do you have faith to believe that God will provide what you need If not why not?

A FRIEND CALLED TIME

15

"The best thing about the future is that it comes only one day at a time."
— Abraham Lincoln

Time is a tool to the person who will dare to use it, but an enemy to the one who pays no attention to it. Throughout this chapter, I will clarify this statement so that time will forever benefit you.

A tool is a device that can be used to produce an item or achieve a task; but it is not consumed in the process. You know this to be true about time. When time is ended, so is life as we know it.

Time is a dreamer's best friend. If a dreamer steps out in faith to activate a dream and broadcast the plan to others, the process of realized expectations has begun.

I am reminded of that great dreamer Martin Luther King Jr., who was not only a clergyman, but also an effective civil rights leader. His leadership and his ability to inspire people of all races have been acknowledged with a Nobel Peace Prize and a national holiday in his honor.

I bring up this great man not to give you a history lesson, but to make a point about time as an ally to a dreamer. My statements here are not opinions or subjective but are based on fact.

On August 28, 1963, Dr. King made a seventeen-minute speech on the steps of the Lincoln Memorial in Washington, D.C., at the culmination of the March on Washington for Jobs and Freedom. Some 200,000 civil rights supporters of all races attended, and thousands listened and watched on TV and radio.

The speech had many revisions and drafts before its delivery. One of its original titles was "Normalcy, Never Again." Once Dr. King gave the speech, those who took a stand were never the same.

Dr. King had a dream of an integrated and unified America where all races and creeds of people would live together in harmony. You say, "We are far from that being a reality," but much has transpired since that speech. Interracial marriage, which was nearly nonexistent, now makes up one in seven marriages. And the United States has its first African American President.

Dr. King was not in a war with institutionalized racism but took a stand that would revolutionize the thinking of all Americans. He dreamed that one day his four children would be judged by the content of their character and not the color of their skin.

"Now is the time" is repeated six times in his speech. God does not tell you everything, but when you dream, you act in faith as if what you are acting on will manifest today. Great dreamers have an assurance that, although success is not instant, it is guaranteed.

If no one took action when they heard the speech, we might still be in the exact same predicament as a nation as we were on August 28, 1963.

Time was Dr. King's friend. He understood dreaming and the possibility and nobility of a dream outliving the dreamer. On April 3, 1968, Dr. King made a speech called "The Mountaintop." In this speech he spoke of the Promised Land and longevity. God had given him the vision of achieving his dream. This reality and the state of America at the time inspired him to inspire others to hold on to what they had heard. He told them that there was a chance that he would not get to the Promised Land with them, but, as a people, they would reach their destination. Twelve hours after the speech, he was silenced by a sniper's bullet.

Dr. King understood time and season. Whether he saw the dream reach fruition did not take away from his knowledge that it would come to pass.

The tool of time is a gift given to you by God. But how you use it determines whether it is your friend or foe.

Simply being punctual to an assigned task or not can either force you into your destiny or keep you stagnant for a long time. When you decide to do the right thing, you have to keep doing it. God is a rewarder to those who are faithful. Make a decision to continue on the right path forever.

Dieters know too well about the tool of time. There was a woman who tried to lose weight for years. She kept telling all who would listen that she did not understand how she could not seem to shed those extra pounds. But years into her quandary, she realized that she had some bad habits. She regularly ate a healthy breakfast, lunch, dinner, and two snacks, but the hours from dusk to bedtime proved to be her enemy. That's when she snacked on fat-laden foods and foods that were hard for her body to digest while she slept. All those hours, days, months, and years of planned eating were wasted in the three- to four-hour period when she threw discipline to the wind.

She was in an unfortunate cycle. However, she realized that she was disciplined and added that discipline to the extended hours before bedtime. Her awakening turned time from an enemy to a friend. She determined to redeem the time she had spent cancelling out her good eating habits by binging during the evening hours. Now, years later, she is closer to her goal weight and is in a much healthier place.

Time is for the disciplined. You cannot operate in time without discipline. If you are climbing the ladder to corporate success, you cannot show up late for work nearly every day. Being dependable is a cornerstone of all successful people.

Ignoring time does not make it go away; it simply turns time into your enemy. Time is just a tool, and you must decide how you are going to use it. If you want to spend it criticizing those you consider to be haters, time is your enemy; but if you spend time bettering yourself, time is your friend.

Time has no personality. It is an asset that God gave you to fulfill His purpose in your life. Everyone gets the same amount: 8,760 hours a year. You are to use it to your advantage. It is not meant for you to dream, be inspired, tell your friends, and then wake up five years later having done nothing but that. Time does not want to be an enemy. It is a God-given tool for everyone to value.

What is stopping you from using your time wisely? Why aren't you working on your dream? God gave everybody something to start with. There is no one on this earth that is empty handed. You do have a dream.

I have come to realize that there is no such thing as "I have nothing." You can spend ten years saying that you have nothing to start your dream with, and that will not change the truth that you do. God says that you do. First, you have the power of your words. There is life and death in what you say. Start there. Say what you want, not what you do not want.

Dr. King's thirty-nine years on this earth were not outstanding because of his great materialistic giving. Although I am sure he gave to many, his ability to invoke and to inspire were his trademarks. He shared his dream and made believers out of those who dared to follow him. His haters played no part in his decision to move forward. Being locked up and hit with rocks did not stop the dream.

What are you holding on to that you can use? Everything that you possess is profitable. If you say that what you have is worth nothing, then that is what it is worth. Whatever you say is what it is.

I am going to refute that saying "It is what it is!" right now. It is what you say it is. If you are sick, then start by saying that you are healed. If you are without employment, stop saying that you are broke. What do you have to sow? Cook a pot of rice and feed your family, or invite someone over to share. Season it up, add some butter, and give God thanks. Start with what you have.

In God's kingdom, opposites are the rule. It's not over till the word comes out that it is finished. When Lazarus died, Jesus purposely took four days just to give God glory in the sight of all those who were there. When he arrived at the gravesite, there were the sisters, fussing at Jesus that he had taken too long. Nevertheless, he told them to remove the stone that sealed the grave. He called for Lazarus to come out, and he did. He instructed those standing around to take off Lazarus's grave clothes and let him go free.

It does not matter how long that you have stood in the same spot; God is imploring you to start now. Rewards come to them that start. It does not matter when you start, just start. If you have wasted time already, forgive yourself and start today.

The same reward will be given to those who started a long time ago and those who start today. You can make yourself be a chosen one by acting now. Change time from an enemy to a friend. This authority is in you.

If you begin today, you will not recognize yourself next year. You will look back and wonder what happened.

A Cobb County, Georgia, school bus driver had this epiphany. A drunk driver killed her daughter in 1993. At the time, the daughter was married and had two children. The bus driver also had a son who was about eight years old. She grieved and grieved the death of her daughter. It did not help that her son-in-law did not bring the grandchildren over regularly. Sometimes a year would go by before she saw them.

Seven years into her depression over the loss of her daughter, she was up early one morning, praying. The Lord spoke to her, "Daughter, are you going to waste the next seven years of your life the same way that you have wasted the past seven years?"

At that moment she realized that she had missed seven crucial years of her young son's life. Standing in front of her was a young man in his last year of being a teenager. He had finished elementary, middle school and was about to graduate high school without the emotional support of his mother. She shook herself, forgave the drunk driver and her son-in-law, and began life from that point, making up for the last seven years by being productive for the future.

God is not going to hold you responsible for the wasted time after you start moving. He just wants your faith, the kind that is only fruitful with activity. As long as you have breath in your body, you have a chance to get up.

God knows how to redeem time. He operates in eternity, but time is in His hand. He is the beginning and the end, the first and the last. He is not leaving all the changes up to you. All he wants is your faith. God does not respond to pity parties, God responds to faith.

Start working to catch up to that dream that you had a long time ago. Time does not hold it against you that you wasted it. Make friends with time today. It is calling for your attention. It does not have a choice but to pass you by if you do not use it. It is your friend if you let it be.

"So the last shall be first, and the first last." – Matthew 20:16

Questions?

In what ways do you feel like you've wasted some time and wasted even more time trying to get it back?

Are you undisciplined? In what ways?

Do you have poor time management skills?

Name three things that you do that wastes time.

Name three ways that time gets out of control for you.

Name three things that you can do to gain control of your time moving forward.

HEADED IN THE RIGHT DIRECTION

16

"Change is the watchword of progression."

— Ella Wheeler Wilcox

You do not want to waste valuable time stumbling from one road to another because you do not have a clue. You know you have been dreaming since you were young; you just never had anyone pushing you to that big dream. Or if you did, you knew that it could not be right. Well, it is right. That big dream was you in your future. It is time to dream again and to walk in the reality of faith fulfilled.

If you read the chapter "Anaconda Dreaming," do not forget the principles in it. Do not downgrade your dream. Your destiny is not just to bless you, but to touch the lives of everyone around you. You are blessed to be a blessing. Remember the anaconda: stunting his growth by keeping him in a small cage also limits his longevity. Don't let your dream die before it is fulfilled. It's God's desire that every dream reach its maximum potential. Never stop believing.

What if you start toward your dream and you are really enjoying the trip, but all the doors close and never reopen? So what? You have lost nothing. You can always go back to doing what you are doing now. Remember the lepers in the Bible who were outside of the city, dying of starvation—but they would be killed if they went into the city because it was unlawful. One day they realized something: "Why are we going to sit here until we die?" They went in and found the city empty (2 Kings 7). They were saved because they took that risk.

You do have a choice. Choosing faith is always the right answer. Just like the lepers in 2 Kings, you can choose to get up and follow your heart. The desire to do bigger has always been with you.

The most important things in your life are God, your family, and your focus. If your heart is not fixed on what God wants you to do, you are perishing already. When you do not have focus, you do not have vision. "And without vision [you] perish" (Proverbs 29:18). To live in God's kingdom, you must go after something. Sitting still is never what you are supposed to be doing.

For years I heard and read the story in Exodus about Moses leading the children of Israel out of Egypt, only for them to have a great sea in front of them. As the people complained that Moses had brought them out of the bondage of Egypt only to have them drown in the Red Sea, Moses began to speak. He told them that they would never see again the enemy that was chasing them. He told them to "stand still and see the salvation of the Lord." But God did not let the story end there. He corrected Moses for telling the people to stand still and told them to go forward (Genesis 14).

Faith without works is dead. You can't stand still and expect to see your dreams come true. You have to keep moving. Move and keep moving forward.

When you live in expectation, your focus changes. You expect God to open the doors for you. You expect your life to change for the better. You live in expectation. You have to keep your focus clear. Never forgot who you are and whose you are. God is the one leading you. It is He that is giving you what your heart desires. That dream is not from the steak and gravy from last night's dinner. If it is, then why does it keep reoccurring?

What you need is a complete change. After you go through your metamorphosis and change into a butterfly, you can no longer hang out with the caterpillars. Have you ever touched the wings of a butterfly? They turn to powder in your hand. That's because they were made for flying, not crawling on the ground. Keep your wings spread and keep flying.

All the changes you have gone through have prepared you for greatness. They were not idle happenings. Use them for what they were meant—to propel you to sit on things higher than where you are. What would the purpose of having wings be, if not but for flying?

Everything that you went through was for your own good. Your trials were not meant to change your name to victim. They are your testimonies for the next level. Since you made it through all that mess and came out victorious, change your mind. You are more than a conqueror. You are destined for greatness.

Check out some of the great leaders of yesterday and today. Do some research. You will find that a number of them had a history of abuse, neglect, and poverty. It did not stop them from gaining success, and does not have to stop you. You can have whatever you say you can have, according to your faith (Mark 11). How much faith do you have? You will never know until you walk it out.

Faith without action is dead faith. Let your faith tell you this: just because you were a victim does not give you the excuse to stay a victim. It happened, but it is not happening now. Get attention for the right reason: "Do you remember how he used to live?" "Isn't that the woman that used to be on crack? Look at her now!" "Didn't he used to live in the projects?" "She was just working at Mickey D's three years ago." "Isn't that the guy whose daddy was in jail when he graduated?" Yeah, that's right! But, look at you now!

You were born to inspire. You were created to be an example of what God can do when faith is activated. You do not have to talk to inspire. Just live your life, and it will speak for you. Or you can tell it! Somebody is waiting to hear your testimony. She needs to know that she can come out of the trouble she's in. He needs to know that he is going to make it.

You are meant to be an inspiration. But, that will never be if you do not dream bigger. Get up and make that move. Start that business, get that degree, begin that ministry, or sacrifice that time and money for those children. The stage is set, and your audience is waiting to be inspired.

The power is in you. All you have to do is turn it on with action. It is not hard. You can do all things because Christ is strengthening you (Philippians 4:13). That dunamis just needs to be lit. Light it up with the Word. Light it up with your faith. Light it up with your plans to go forward.

And don't just sit there. Do something! God is going to do greater than you ever expected. You are stronger than you think, but you will never know until you try. You want to prove how strong you are? Give your weakness to God. His strength is made perfect in your weakness (II Cor. 12:9).

You will never know His strength just by studying these words. You have to be a doer and not just a hearer (James 1:22-25). You can rehearse it and rehearse it, but until you put some action to it, it is just words. God is going to exceed your maximum, just by your continued movement. I can't emphasize any more than this. Just try, and you'll find out that it is true.

You have to think multiplication. If you do not, you will always be fighting a losing battle. You have to expect more. God promises to give you a greater percentage than what you put out. The Kingdom Bank is the best place to invest. You can read all about it, but the only way multiplication takes place is when you activate your ability to give. This is faith giving. This is not gambling in the casino.

This is not going to the track every Saturday. This is not a poker game. This is God's guarantee to His children, of whom you are one.

Put seed to your dreams, and watch them grow. Sow into what you want God to do for you. He's in the business of expansion. His kingdom is going to cover the earth. Don't you want to be part of this great takeover?

Keep these words in your mouth. Any other sound will be a hindrance to your growth. If you make sounds that do not blend with prosperity, you will always be on the other side of the fence, just looking in. It is God's pleasure to give you the kingdom (Luke 12:32).

Prosperity and poverty do not blend. They are like oil and water. You can mix them, shake them as hard as you can, put them in the blender—and it still will not matter. When they settle, the oil will always be on top. It's the same with poverty and prosperity. Prosperity will always be on top. The sound of prosperity is heaven's sound. If you keep that sound around you, you will always attract prosperity.

God wants your prosperity to include all of you: body, soul and spirit. God does not want you just to accept Jesus as your savior and sit around waiting to go to the place He is preparing for you. What will you do for the years between your salvation on earth and the day you leave here? Salvation is derived from the word soltare, which means, among other things, prosperity and well-being.

Make the right sound. Talk the right words, and live with the right aura. The arena of prosperity is God's kingdom here on earth. Join those that have crossed from poverty into the sound of prosperity.

Waiting for you on the other side is a group of friends that you will never meet until you are there. God ordains friends. God called Abraham his friend three times. Abraham was not perfect, but his faith in God put him in right standing with Him. God wants relationship. You are made in His image, so you naturally act like Him; you desire good relationships too. A friend striving for success just like you is an invaluable asset.

Friends can either help you up or tear you down. Who are you with? No matter how hard you try to bring yourself up, if you put yourself with bad company, you will neglect all your good training. Friends love at all times and were created to handle adversity.

Seek friends who will challenge you. Seek friends who do not mind you trying to achieve what they already have. Expand your mind, and look for friends that are going where you are going, are already there, or want to go where you are headed. There is strength in numbers.

I want to make sure you understand this last point: God has never changed

His mind about you. The dream that is waiting to be fulfilled by you is still there. You may have watched someone else walk right into the place that you thought was for you. It is still for you. This universe is big enough for everyone's big dream. It does not matter if you are twelve or ninety-nine, start the process. As long as there is strength in your body, you can do it.

Caleb was eighty-plus years old when he proclaimed that he still could handle his inheritance. He had spied out the Promised Land some forty years before, heard ten of the twelve spies give bad reports about the Promised Land, and watched most of his peers die in the wilderness. None of that mattered. The dream he had waited for all his life was days away from reality. God had sustained Caleb, and he wanted what was promised to him and God's people (Joshua 14).

The covenant is still here. God is a God of His word. Your big dream is still waiting for your faithful work to meet with opportunity. Keep dreaming big, and never give up.

REFLECTIONS FOR DREAMERS

17

"Yes, you can be a dreamer and a doer too, if you will remove one word from your vocabulary: impossible."

— Robert H. Schuller

I t is said that the difference between a dream and a goal is a plan. As you make your plan now, remember that there is a direction for you if you want to achieve all your goals. For plans to be accomplished, you must keep your dream alive with activity.

In this final chapter, I will give you some points to study. In conjunction with knowing that God wants you to have good success, practicing these points will encourage the fruition of your dream.

I urge you to read this book again and again until the information meshes with your spirit and you begin to live differently. You must conceive that God has a plan already prepared for you. You have only to acknowledge Him and believe what He says about you. Yes, it is for you. Yes, you were born for more than this.

Today, begin to venture out into your enlarged territory: start that business, expand that business, write that book, ask for that promotion, enroll in school, start that ministry. You know what you hear. And God knows the thoughts He has for you; He just wants you to be made aware and to walk and blend with them. You are hearing His voice today.

Illumination

You are never going to launch forward if your mind is not illuminated. Focus on what you want, and don't even mention what you do not want. A new driver is taught to watch the road in front, not on the sides. That's because you go in the direction you're looking. If you look to the right, you will go right.

Do Not Believe the Hype—Keep Dreaming

You have stepped out in faith, and you are watching your dream come into focus right now. All of your supporters are patting you on the back and saying what a fine job you have done. You can't seem to find much negative press. Now is not the time to gloat. If you have reached a pinnacle, start looking for the next one. Your dream is not fulfilled until you are no longer where you are now. In every round you go higher and higher. Each step is a new beginning. What will you do in five years when your current dream has been realized? Dreamers keep dreaming.

Friends Will Leave

Humans have a habit of attaching themselves to people—even to their own detriment. It is good to have friends, and God expects you to have friends. But be aware that friends can attach themselves to you, and you can find yourself depending on them to always be there.

Friends come for different reasons. Some friendships last a lifetime, but the majority of friendships are either seasonal or for a reason. The Lord knows what you need before you ask. Keep a friendly disposition, and you will always have friends.

When a friendship is made, benefit from it as much as you can while you can. Lifetime friends are not going to leave. Even distance cannot shake their loyalty. But there are those you may have only while you are on one phase of your dream. And there are friends that may stay a bit longer.

Some friends will leave unexpectedly. Do not despair. The adversity of some circumstances may be too much for them to bear. But the "down for life" friends will remain. Put all your trust in God, and He will guide you to the right friends to hold dear.

All your friends will not fit into your dream. You do not know all that tomorrow holds. If they are your friends today, thank God. When it is time for them to leave, rest in God. He knows what's best for you.

Be More Dedicated to God than People

As you grow in grace and your dream begins to expand, you may feel obligated to your supporters. Do not be more loyal to them than you are to God. Keep your spiritual relationship strong. Supporters are not gods. They know some things but can't lead you down every road.

The supporters who are closest to you can cause the most harm.

Remember it is God who gives you the power to get wealth (Deut. 8:18). If you put your dependence on what people can do for you, your faith is weak.

Too many superstars have neglected the truth and started believing the hype. Thank your supporters, honor them, and continue to dream. You are not acting aloof. The truth is that they should be dreaming too.

Unfortunately, some supporters are there for the wrong reason. They enjoy the attention of the hype. Do not judge them, but encourage them to dream just like you.

No More Excuses

You can always find a reason why something will not work. For every positive there has to be a negative. But why focus on the negative? You will miss out on so many miracles with pessimistic beliefs. If you believe that the plan will work, it will. If you make a mistake, great! Remember, dreamers have to have failures under their belt.

You do not want the time spent on reading this book to have been a waste. Toss your excuses out of the window.

After you have embraced the dream and made goals, don't find an excuse to skip a step that seems too difficult. There is nothing too hard for God. You can make it, and you can do this. It is the small things that spoil big things.

Do not let haters influence your thinking. Separate yourself from the faithless. Silence the voices of the past that said you could not do this or that. Quiet the voice inside yourself that says, "I can't." You are your own worst enemy.

Get up every day and speak over yourself. Tell yourself what God says about you. Family, friends, and supporters should serve as a confirmation of what you already know about what God says about you.

Excuse is a word in the dictionary simply because everyone can have one. But you must believe that only diligence brings abundance. Be vigilant. Be unstoppable. Live in optimism. And "be strong in the Lord and the power of His might" (Ephesians 6:10). Translation: Be strong because you have been empowered to do all you are called to do.

"Finally, my brethren, be strong in the Lord and in the power of His might."
– Ephesians 6:10

ABOUT THE AUTHOR

Anthony Murray a prolific energetic Pastor and Author delivers the word of God with humor and practical knowledge which enables people to apply it to their everyday lives. Anthony Murray is definitely not your ordinary Pastor.

Anthony Murray is building a 3D church, a multi generational, multi-cultural, and futuristic generation of believers. The 3D-Church is relevant to the times and activities going on in the world today. Heaven is not divided into class, race, or age so why should the church be on Sundays.

> *"Today's generation crosses racial lines, age, class and sexual orientation. God's Word is for everyone. God is pouring His spirit on all people. The harvest is ripe but the laborers are few. I believe God has called me to a generation of people who are not weak-minded Christians but Christians with a take-over mentality. We have one Great Commission which is to win souls and make disciples of Jesus Christ. "* –Anthony Murray

While a Youth Pastor, God called him to create Club VFL, one of the fastest growing and largest youth ministries in Atlanta GA. With the blessing of his father/pastor, in 2006, he started Oasis Family Life Church. He now oversees one of the fastest growing churches in Paulding County Georgia.

Anthony Murray has a philanthropist's spirit. He trusts in the good works of charities. He considers giving with one's finances, gifts, time and talents the most effective avenue of proving our belief and trust in God. He supports both local and global organizations such as Habitat for Humanity, March of Dimes, Susan G. Komen Foundation, Compassion International and more. His philosophy is "God is into People who are into People"

Anthony Murray is married to Christina Murray. They have two daughters and currently reside in the Atlanta Metro Area.